Briefly:
Fletcher's *Situation Ethics:*
The New Morality

The SCM Briefly series

Anselm's *Proslogion* (with the Replies of Gaunilo and Anselm)
Aquinas' *Summa Theologica Part 1* (God, Part I)
Aquinas' *Summa Theologica Part 2* (God, Part II)
Aristotle's *The Nicomachean Ethics*
Ayer's *Language, Truth and Logic*
Bentham's *An Introduction to the Principles of Morals and Legislation*
Descartes' *Meditations on First Philosophy*
Fletcher's *Situation Ethics: The New Morality*
Hume's *Dialogues Concerning Natural Religion*
Hume's *An Enquiry Concerning Human Understanding*
Kant's *Critique of Practical Reason (The Concept of the Highest Good and the Postulates of the Practical Reason)*
Kant's *Groundwork of the Metaphysics of Morals*
Kant's *Religion within the Boundaries of Mere Reason*
Kierkegaard's *Fear and Trembling*
Mill's *On Liberty*
Mill's *Utilitarianism*
Moore's *Principia Ethica*
Nietzsche's *Beyond Good and Evil*
Plato's *The Republic*
Russell's *The Problems of Philosophy*
Sartre's *Existentialism and Humanism*

Briefly: 25 Great Philosophers from Plato to Sartre

Other Books by David Mills Daniel published by SCM Press:

SCM AS/A2 Ethics and Moral Philosophy
SCM Revision Guide: AS/A2 Ethics and Religious Ethics
SCM Revision Guide: AS/A2 Philosophy of Religion

Briefly: Fletcher's *Situation Ethics: The New Morality*

David Mills Daniel

scm press

© David Mills Daniel 2009

Published in 2009 by SCM Press
Editorial office
13–17 Long Lane,
London, ECIA 9PN, UK

SCM Press is an imprint of Hymns Ancient and Modern Ltd
(a registered charity)
St Mary's Works, St Mary's Plain,
Norwich, NR3 3BH, UK
www.scm-canterburypress.co.uk

The author and publisher acknowledge material reproduced from
Joseph Fletcher, *Situation Ethics: The New Morality*, London: SCM
Press, 1966. All rights reserved.

British Library Cataloguing in Publication data

A catalogue record for this book is available
from the British Library

978 0 334 04176 4

Typeset by Regent Typesetting, London
Printed and bound by
Bookmarque, Croydon, Surrey

Contents

Introduction   vii

Context   I

Who was Joseph Fletcher?   I
What is *Situation Ethics*?   2
Some Key Quotations   25
Suggestions for Further Reading   30

Detailed Summary of Joseph Fletcher's *Situation Ethics: The New Morality*   33

Foreword   33
I   Three Approaches   34
II   Some Presuppositions   38
III   Love Only Is Always Good   43
IV   Love Is the Only Norm   46
V   Love and Justice Are the Same   49
VI   Love Is Not Liking   53
VII   Love Justifies Its Means   56
VIII Love Decides There and Then   59
IX   Postscriptum: Why?   62

X   An Appendix: Two Other Corruptions and
        Four Cases   65
Overview   69

Glossary   91
Index   115

Introduction

The SCM *Briefly* series is designed to enable students and general readers to acquire knowledge and understanding of key texts in philosophy, philosophy of religion, theology and ethics. While the series will be especially helpful to those following university and A-level courses in philosophy, ethics and religious studies, it will in fact be of interest to anyone looking for a short guide to the ideas of a particular philosopher or theologian.

Each book in the series takes a piece of work by one philosopher and provides a summary of the original text, which adheres closely to it, and contains direct quotations from it, thus enabling the reader to follow each development in the philosopher's argument(s). Throughout the summary, there are page references to the original philosophical writing, so that the reader has ready access to the primary text. In the Introduction to each book, you will find details of the edition of the philosophical work referred to.

In *Briefly: Fletcher's Situation Ethics*, we refer to Joseph Fletcher, *Situation Ethics: The New Morality*, London: SCM Press, 1966.

Each *Briefly* begins with an Introduction, followed by a chapter on the Context in which the work was written. Who was this writer? Why was this book written? With Some Key Quotations and some Suggestions for Further Reading,

Introduction

this *Briefly* aims to get anyone started in their philosophical investigation. The Detailed Summary of the philosophical work is followed by a concise chapter-by-chapter Overview and an extensive Glossary and Index of terms.

Bold type is used in the Detailed Summary and Overview sections to indicate the first occurrence of words and phrases that appear in the Glossary. The Glossary also contains terms used elsewhere in this *Briefly* guide and other terms that readers may encounter in their study of Fletcher's *Situation Ethics*.

Context

Who was Joseph Fletcher?

The theologian and ethicist Joseph Francis Fletcher was born in 1905, in East Orange, New Jersey, but following his parents' separation he moved with his mother to West Virginia. After attending West Virginia University, he studied at Berkeley Divinity School (now part of Yale University), Yale University and the London School of Economics, where he was a student of R. H. Tawney. Ordained into the (Anglican) Episcopal Church of America, he was dean of St Paul's Cathedral, Cincinnati (1936–44), and then taught Christian ethics and business ethics at the Episcopal Divinity School, Cambridge, Massachusetts, and Harvard University (1944–70), during which time he wrote his popular and controversial book, *Situation Ethics: The New Morality* (1966).

Passionately interested in social justice, Fletcher was an active campaigner for workers' rights and for the improvement of working conditions, and one of his first books was *The Church and Industry* (1930). He had a long association with the union movement in the United States, going back to his work, during his student days, for the United Mine Workers of America. Along with other academics, he was accused by Senator Joseph McCarthy of supporting communism during the 'witch-hunt' for communist sympathizers in the 1950s.

Fletcher is also recognized as one of the pioneers of bio-ethics, and from 1970 until his retirement in 1983 he was Professor of Medical Ethics at the University of Virginia. His *Morals and Medicine* (1954) reflects his belief that there is nothing inherently superior in natural processes as opposed to those devised by human beings. An advocate of birth control, planned pregnancy and sterilization, and of voluntary euthanasia, he was actively involved in such organizations as the Planned Parenthood Federation, the Association for the Study of Abortion, the American Eugenics Society (The Society for the Study of Social Biology) and the Euthanasia Society of America (The Society for the Right to Die), of which he was President (1974–76). His first wife, Forrest Hatfield, was also a campaigner for birth control and an associate of Margaret Sanger, founder of the American Birth Control League (later the Planned Parenthood Federation).

In the 1960s, Fletcher renounced his Christian belief and became a humanist, although he maintained his links with the Episcopal Church and religious groups. A prolific author of books and articles, his other writings include *William Temple: Twentieth Century Christian* (1963), *Moral Responsibility: Situation Ethics at Work* (1967), *The Ethics of Genetic Control: Ending Reproductive Roulette* (1974) and *Joseph Fletcher: Memoirs of An Ex-Radical* (published posthumously in 1993). He died in 1991.

What is *Situation Ethics?*

The source of situation ethics

The point of departure for Fletcher's book is Jesus' words, as recorded in Mark's Gospel (12.28–31):

What is Situation Ethics?

> And one of the scribes ... asked him, 'Which command-
> ment is the first of all?' Jesus answered, 'The first is, "Hear,
> O Israel: The Lord our God, the Lord is one; and you shall
> love the Lord your God with all your heart, and with all
> your soul ... and with all your strength." The second is
> this, "You shall love your neighbour as yourself." There is
> no other commandment greater than these.'

The normative ethical theory of situation ethics, or situationism, is based on this affirmation by Jesus of the 'Christian
love ethic' or the 'law of love'. But what does it mean in practice? How should we apply it in actual situations? However
inspiring we may find Jesus' words, trying to be as loving as
possible towards our neighbour(s), or trying to increase the
amount of love in the world, seems a rather vague ethical
principle. And this is a serious problem with situation ethics.
The theory and Fletcher's book were fashionable and controversial, when they appeared in the 1960s; and they continue
to be interesting and challenging today; but they both suffer
from the same vagueness as the love ethic itself.

Three approaches to ethical decisions

However, this is an important part of Fletcher's argument. As
(he insists) no situation requiring an ethical response is ever
exactly the same as another, there is never a right course of
action, which fits all (or even every type of) situation(s). This
means that, of the three main ways of making ethical decisions which Fletcher describes (Chapter 1), the legalistic, the
antinomian and the situational, only the third is appropriate
to the complexity of ethical issues. So, what are these three
ethical approaches?

3

Context

Legalistic ethics

The ethical legalist views every ethical decision from the perspective of a fixed set of rules and regulations, such as those derived from traditional Christian teaching, which he feels bound to apply to every issue. In Christianity (Fletcher explains), Roman Catholic legalism has taken the form of natural law ethics, with moralists working out ethical rules by applying reason to the facts of nature, and producing what they claim to be universally valid 'natural' moral laws. Protestant legalism has followed the Bible, and based equally inflexible ethical rules on the teachings of the Old Testament prophets, the words of Jesus, or the writings of the evangelists and apostles. The attraction of ethical legalism is that it simplifies ethical decisions, because there is always a rule to apply. Its drawback is its rigidity, which may lead to mistaken ethical priorities: Fletcher agrees with Bertrand Russell's comment that Christian ethical legalists tend (wrongly) to regard adultery as more immoral than political corruption, despite the fact that the effects of the latter are much more damaging.

Antinomianism

This approach is the opposite of the first, as it dispenses with principles altogether. Some Christians believe that through grace, and the new life in Christ that they have received as a result of salvation through faith, ethical rules no longer apply to them. The heresy of Gnosticism (knowledge) involved the belief that some people have special knowledge, and will just know what is right. This approach rejects all general moral principles, so ethical decisions become matters of intuition: in consequence they are spontaneous, but also erratic.

4

What is Situation Ethics?

Situationism

The situationist, however, avoids the extremes of both legalism and antinomianism. He treats his community's ethical values and principles with respect, because he realizes that they can shed light on ethical problems, but he refuses to make them into an ethical straitjacket. He is prepared to set them aside in a particular situation, if he thinks that doing so is the most loving action. For the situationist, self-sacrificing, neighbour-centred love, the Christian *agape*, is the only absolute ethical standard. Any other general principles derive from, and are subordinate to, it. The situationist's ethical decisions and actions reflect his awareness that circumstances alter cases, and that he must apply the love ethic in a way which acknow-ledges that no two situations are exactly alike.

There are no absolute ethical rules

But, there seems to be an inconsistency here with what Fletcher has said about the value of the community's general ethical principles. If no two situations are ever exactly alike, and the only principle that matters is the law of love, how can the situationist make use of general principles? Surely, he must ignore all general ethical principles, and concentrate on trying to do the most loving thing in each unique ethical situation? For example, the general ethical principles of most communi-ties prohibit murder and theft, but, as Fletcher makes clear, they are not ruled out for the situationist. In fact, any general ethical principles are to be applied in accordance with what Fletcher calls the policy of 'principled relativism'. They provide only insights and guidance: in no sense are they to be regarded as definite ethical rules, because only love really matters.

Thus, the anti-Nazi German theologian Dietrich Bonhoeffer was executed for trying to kill Hitler. In his particular situation, doing so was the right action to perform, even though it clashed with the fundamental Christian principle prohibiting murder, because the cause of love would have been served by removing Hitler, and so ending Nazi barbarism and World War Two. However, it could be argued that Fletcher's example merely highlights the fact that, as R. M. Hare points out, principles can be universal, without being general. What complex ethical dilemmas require is not an attempt to apply a very general principle, such as 'do not kill' or 'do not steal', but a more precise formulation of these principles, to cover situations where killing or stealing may be ethically justified. The rightness of trying to kill Hitler could be formulated as a universal ethical principle, along the lines that 'no moral agent should ever try to kill another person, except where it is obvious that killing him will eliminate a barbaric system of government, or bring a war to an end, or save many other lives'. Simply to describe the act of killing a particular person as the most loving thing to do in a particular situation obscures the reason which justifies killing in that situation, but not in another.

Being a situationist

To illustrate how situationism works in practice, Fletcher recounts a situation in a United States' mental hospital, where a young unmarried female patient with a radical schizophrenic psychosis has been raped by another patient. Her father wants an immediate abortion, but state law only allows it on 'therapeutic' grounds: where the mother's life is at risk. What would the situationist's attitude be? Fletcher maintains that the law of love requires an abortion, for the sake of the patient's physical and mental well-being, irrespective of whether or not her life is in danger. He adds that the situationist would argue that abortion, in this situation, is not killing, because there is no person or human life in an embryo at an early stage of pregnancy.

Many people would agree with Fletcher and the father that an abortion would be justified. But, Fletcher does not explore the reasons for taking this view. Those who regard abortion as the most loving response to this situation would maintain that the interests of the suffering girl should take precedence over those (if any) of the unborn embryo/foetus. However, one reason why Roman Catholic ethicists are likely to disagree, given that the girl's life does not seem to be at risk, is rejection of Fletcher's view that an embryo, at an early stage of pregnancy, is not a person and lacks intrinsic value. Views on the rights and wrongs of abortion hinge on this all-important issue of whether or not an embryo/foetus has moral status; but Fletcher does not discuss it.

Four working principles

Fletcher (Chapter II) suggests four principles that will help situationists to make the right ethical decisions in each unique situation.

Pragmatism

This is to do with what works, and achieving a successful outcome to problems. It does not provide ethical principles or standards; we have to choose these for ourselves. But, approaching ethical problems in a practical, common-sense way enables situationists to take account of all the aspects and complexities of a situation, and to apply the principle of love effectively to it.

Relativism

No two situations are ever identical, so situationists should avoid words like 'never'. For the Christian situationist, the absolute norm, or ultimate criterion, is agapeic love, which must always be applied, but also made relative to the actual situation. Further, situationists must never make a subordinate principle, which may be helpful in one situation, into an absolute rule which they always apply.

Positivism

Although reason is important in ethical decisions, it has its limits. Fundamental ethical principles cannot be proved, so they are decisions, not conclusions. The Christian ethicist cannot prove that love is the fundamental moral principle, any more than utilitarians, like Bentham or Mill, could prove that pleasure is the highest good. Fletcher agrees with the accepted interpretation of the famous passage in Hume's *A Treatise of Human Nature* that there is a logical gap between facts and values: no ethical decision is ever logically compelled by any statement of fact. Thus, there is no logically necessary step from a statement like 'these people are starving' to the conclusion 'we must (try to) feed them'. Ethical choices cannot be proved, verified or validated, only vindicated by their success in practice. Thus, the Christian ethicist adopts *agape* love as his key principle and his highest good, when in faith, and on the basis of what he sees in Christ, he affirms that God is love.

8

What is Situation Ethics?

Personalism

In situation ethics, people, not things, are what matter, and there are no inherent values which do not relate to human needs. Immorality arises when the formulation of Kant's categorical imperative, that people should always be treated as ends, never merely as means, is ignored, and people are used and things are loved. In Christian ethics, the central importance of persons is reinforced by belief that God is personal, and has created human beings in his own image. Situation ethics is not concerned with what is (inherently) good, but with how to do the most loving thing possible in a particular situation.

Conscience

For situationists, conscience is a function, not a faculty. It is a way of describing the attempt to make creative and constructive ethical decisions. The situationist does not see the role of conscience as being to review and condemn past ethical decisions, but to help make the right decisions, in the present and future.

Only love is always good

Fletcher (Chapter III) insists that we must free ourselves of any idea that there are any values that are independent of doing the most loving thing to persons. And, it is circumstances which determine what is the most loving thing. No action, thing or state of affairs has any value in itself; but only because it happens to help persons (and is good) or to hurt them (and is bad). Even accepted and apparently self-evident

9

ethical principles, such as helping those in distress, may fail by the test of what is the most loving action in one, particular situation: while it may be right, in one situation, to lend money to a father who needs it for his hungry family, it may be wrong in another, for example if the father is a compulsive gambler or an alcoholic.

Love is not a property

There are no ethical properties, either natural, such as pleasure or happiness, or non-natural and known by means of intuition, which a thing or action must possess in order to be good or right. Love is not any kind of substance, but something we do. We must so conduct ourselves that more loving-kindness occurs, through our actions, than through any possible alternatives; and this means following Jesus' example and loving our neighbours.

Nothing is absolute

Coming to terms with the fact that long-accepted ethical rules are relative, not absolute, is hard. Fletcher takes the widely held moral rule that lying is always wrong. This must be rejected: it all depends on the situation. Lying may or may not be the most loving thing to do. Someone may only be able to keep a secret by lying, and would be right to do so, depending upon how loving the action is. Situationism rejects legalism and the view that any principle, including life or truth, is good as such: only love is.

What is Situation Ethics?

Love is the only norm

Thus (Chapter IV), Christian situation ethics dispenses with a rigid system of ethical rules, and replaces it with the law of love. In so doing it emulates Jesus, who ignored the rules of Sabbath observance in order to heal the sick and meet human needs. This does not mean blanket rejection of religious laws, but accepting that they should only be followed if doing so maximizes love.

The Ten Commandments and the Sermon on the Mount

Many of the Ten Commandments, such as those prohibiting killing, stealing and false witness, seem fundamental to a civilized society, but for the situationist they are relative: love may require him to break any or all of them. Christians, in particular, must not make Jesus' ethical teachings, as they are presented in the Sermon on the Mount (Matthew 5—7), into a book of ethical rules. They must recognize that Christian ethics is a situation ethic, and that non-reciprocal, neighbour-regarding, agapeic love, which embraces everybody, including enemies, is the only ethical principle that counts.

But again, Fletcher seems to minimize the importance of fundamental moral principles, such as those which prohibit murder or theft, without explaining the circumstances in which application of the law of love would justify modifying or suspending them.

Criticisms of situation ethics

Fletcher confronts the claim that situation ethics requires more intelligence, factual information and commitment to doing the right thing than most people can manage. However (he insists), these demands are just a fact of life: ethical decisions often are difficult. Christians need to be ethically mature, and willing to take responsibility. *Agape* love rules out selfishness, indifference and exclusive preoccupation with individual concerns. And there can be no escape into a set of ethical rules, in order to escape the challenges and complexities of responsible decision-making. Thus, classical pacifism, which holds that violence is always wrong, in any situation, is a form of legalism. By inflexible application of this principle, pacifists escape having to make the kind of difficult decisions about whether or not to join in or support a war, which situationists cannot evade.

Love and justice

For Fletcher (Chapter V), Christian love must be applied carefully to each situation, so that it becomes justice. However, he redefines justice to fit in with Christian situation ethics. If justice is giving our neighbours their due, what is due to them is love, so love is justice, and justice is love. And, to be just and loving, we must calculate carefully how, in each situation, we can distribute love as widely, and to as many recipients, as possible. Christians must also think in terms of neighbours, not just a neighbour, otherwise *agape* will be reduced to a merely one-to-one relationship.

Christian theologians have been too ready (Fletcher believes) to make love and justice alternatives. For example, Reinhold Niebuhr regarded love as transcendent and unattainable, but justice as relative and attainable. But, instead of saying that love is ideal and justice is actual, we should say that love is maximum justice and justice is optimum love. Again, to talk of rights as what is due to the neighbour can be misleading. What the neighbour has a right to is what is loving; and all so-called 'rights', including such fundamental ones as religious freedom, free speech, the vote, even life itself, are relative, not absolute, and validated only by love.

But, this does not seem at all satisfactory. Does it make sense to justify or defend basic human rights or freedoms, which relate to the intrinsic worth and dignity of each individual, on the grounds of love? And: whose love? Is my right to life or free speech justified only by God's love, or that of other people? Fletcher's argument could be used to justify a government removing these rights and freedoms, if it thought that doing so was the most loving action: a convenient argument for totalitarian states.

Following utilitarianism's example

Situation ethicists (Fletcher argues) can take over the principle of 'the greatest good of the greatest number' from Bentham and Mill. They can substitute *agape* for the pleasure principle, and replace the hedonistic calculus with the agapeic one, with the aim of promoting the greatest amount of neighbour welfare for the largest possible number of neighbours. He accepts that situationism is a consequentialist or teleological ethical theory, as it is directed to maximizing the good of love. However, it can also be understood within a deontological or duty ethical framework: the situationist's duty is to try to achieve the most love possible in every situation.

However, as act utilitarians have found, calculating the consequences of actions is difficult, if not impossible. Certainly, to take one of Fletcher's examples, the situationist's love calculus can throw out some unexpected results, such as

President Truman's decision to drop nuclear bombs on Hiroshima and Nagasaki.

Agapeic love is benevolence

Fletcher (Chapter VI) points out that unlike ordinary love, which involves emotion or affection, agapeic love is primarily a matter of will; so, also unlike feelings, it can be commanded. Whereas we cannot command ourselves to feel emotionally attracted to another person, we can command ourselves to behave in an agapeic or caring way towards other people. Thus, while the opposite of ordinary love is hatred, the opposite of agapeic love is indifference: not caring about the well-being of others. Agapeic love can be defined as benevolence or active goodwill which reaches out to neighbours, not, ultimately, for our sake or theirs, but for God's.

Anyone and everyone is our neighbour

Agapeic love does not expect any return, and so embraces not just the friend, acquaintance and stranger-neighbour but the enemy-neighbour, too. This is what Jesus is talking about in the Sermon on the Mount, when he urges his listeners to be perfect as their heavenly Father is: not 'perfect', in the sense of their love having the completeness of God's, but being all-inclusive, as God's is.

Self-love and neighbour love

While *agape* is essentially other-regarding, reaching out to the neighbour, there is nothing inherently wrong with its being self-regarding, provided it maximizes love: if serving the self rather than one's neighbour means that many neighbours are served, that is the right course of action. Fletcher gives the example of a doctor at a train accident. He should take care of himself, and not risk his own life to rescue one victim trapped in a carriage, as his medical expertise may save the lives of ten other victims. Although it is wrong to love ourselves for our own sake, it is right to love ourselves for our neighbour's and ultimately for God's.

Calculation is not wrong

Successful moral choices involve applying the principle of love effectively to concrete situations, and this requires cool, intelligent assessment, as well as a loving attitude. Only those who are (foolishly) sentimental about love consider the calculation of a situation to be cold or cruel. Again, contrary to what some Christian ethicists contend, it is not the case that the end does not justify the means. This would amount to saying that something useful and loving is not worth what it costs.

Means and ends

Indeed Fletcher maintains that (Chapter VII) unless we have some purpose or end in view, towards which our actions are directed, they are meaningless. Our prime concern is the end we seek, which is to maximize love in a particular situation, so the means we use are of secondary importance. However, they must be appropriate to our end. They are not simply neutral tools, which are ethically indifferent, and must be selected carefully. As with principles or actions, which can be right or wrong according to the circumstances, a means which is good in some situations may be evil in others: it all depends on the situation.

But, again, this seems inconsistent. If the situation is sovereign, and the end justifies the means, can any means be ruled out as inappropriate, provided it works and achieves the desired end? It appears not, as Fletcher's reference to the use of nuclear bombs against Japan in 1945 suggests.

Nothing is intrinsically wrong

Indeed, this is what Fletcher goes on to say: the nature of situation ethics is that anything and everything may be right or wrong, according to the situation. Thus, the situation ethicist will avoid the trap into which the defenders of an intrinsic theory of value fall, as they have to condemn certain acts as intrinsically wrong, even if there are circumstances which make them the appropriate means of maximizing love. Fletcher gives the example of telling a lie to prevent someone committing suicide, or stealing someone's gun to prevent him shooting another person. The moral absolutists, who issue a blanket ban on lying or stealing, may, by condemning them, prevent people committing a lesser evil which could lead to a much greater good. An evil means does not invariably nullify a good end: it is a matter of the proportions of good and evil, and the situation itself. But, the proportions of good and evil are what matter, requiring the exercise of very careful judgement.

However, while this sounds fine in theory, in practice the situationist confronts the same problem as the act utilitarian. Is he really going to be able to calculate all the consequences of his action? Can he be certain, as G. E. Moore warned in

Principia Ethica, that his judgement of the situation will be sufficiently accurate to justify his setting aside common-sense moral rules, which have been shown to work for generations?

Four factors the situationist must take into account

To assist situationists' ethical decisions, Fletcher stipulates four questions they should always ask. What is the end? By what means is it to be achieved? What is the motive? And what are the foreseeable consequences? He pinpoints a defect of traditional ethics, which holds that to be wrong an action needs to fail only one of these tests, but to be right must pass all four. The situationist, on the other hand, considers all ends and means to be interrelated, so that nothing is intrinsically good except the highest good: love. An action may fail one or more of the tests, but still be the most loving in the circumstances, and therefore the right one.

Fletcher dismisses an argument that traditional moralists, and G. E. Moore, raise against this cavalier approach to established moral rules: even if, by flouting the rule in this situation, you do the right thing, what about your example, which may discredit established moral rules in the eyes of others? They may copy you, and get it spectacularly wrong. This generalization (Fletcher believes) is just an antisituational gambit, designed to undermine individual responsibility, and ensure that traditional morality prevails. Love's job is to calculate an action's gains and losses, and then decide what is right. For example, in a particular situation, one family's well-being may be best served by divorce (as perhaps Fletcher's own family's had been), whereas another's may not be.

Love and freedom

Fletcher (Chapter VIII) recognizes that many people do not want the freedom and responsibility which situation ethics gives them. They feel more comfortable with a set of rules which will tell them what to do in every situation. But, the situationist delights in being liberated from the restrictions of moral rules. He prefers to be a free individual, with all the challenges and uncertainties that go with freedom. Of course, as society and the ethical issues it throws up become more complex, the attractions of established rules seem stronger; but, whatever the ethical legalist thinks, it is a mistake to believe that a list of ethical rules can offer relief from the burden of responsible moral decision-making.

Jesus' situation ethic

Although this was much truer of the 1950s and 1960s, when he was developing his ethical theory, Fletcher deplores the hypocrisy, masquerading as moral consensus, which pays lip-service to so-called 'ethical laws', which are then continually broken in practice because they are too petty or rigid to fit the facts of life. Contemporary Christians need to appreciate that the only view of Jesus' ethics consistent with his actual teaching is that he was a situation ethicist. For example, he says nothing about sexual ethics, apart from condemning adultery and divorce, so whether any particular form of sexual relationship, such as homosexuality, is right or wrong must be judged on the basis of his teaching that love is the only thing that matters. Thus, extra-marital relations are not wrong unless they involve people hurting themselves, their partners, or others.

But, would an individual who wanted to commit adultery really ask himself if it was the most loving thing to do (the term seems almost self-contradictory in this context), or simply use situationism as a cover for indulging his desires? And, does Fletcher do justice to the Christian tradition, which rules out certain kinds of sexual activity as never being genuine manifestations of Christian love?

Taking account of an action's total context

For Fletcher, an action's rightness (lovingness) cannot be judged in isolation: it must be evaluated in the light of all the aspects of each unique situation. He draws a parallel with ecology, which studies the relationship between an organism and its environment. Situation ethics is an ecological ethics: it takes account of the total environment of every moral decision. The situationist may be unable to answer such hypothetical questions as: should a husband lie to his wife; desert his family; or not report an item in his tax return? He will probably counter with one of his own: does the questioner have a concrete situation in mind?

However, it is hard to see why the situationist's answer could not be: 'In general, you should do so and so, because experience has shown it to be the most loving conduct, but you must assess each situation, in case there are morally relevant differences.' And this would be more consistent with what Fletcher says about the situationist respecting his community's general ethical principles.

Neocasuistry

For Fletcher (Chapter IX), the pragmatism and relativism of situation ethics offers a new approach to casuistry, which is the process of working out detailed ethical rules to cover specific situations. And it is one which focuses on the particular situation, with a view to maximizing love: agapeic love, seeking to act lovingly towards the neighbour, examines the facts of a situation, and decides what ought to be done. Christian situation ethics must rely upon God's grace; have the law of love as its absolute standard; ensure that there is full knowledge of the facts; and exercise careful, responsible judgement.

Can anyone be a situation ethicist?

Fletcher discusses Christian situation ethics, but acknowledges that lovingness is often the motivating force behind non-Christian and even atheist ethical decisions. Christians do not have a monopoly of love and its power: through the Holy Spirit, it can operate in those who do not know God. However, Christian love is special, as it involves gratitude to God for what he has done for human beings, in particular through Jesus Christ. God does not need our service, but our only way of serving him, and of expressing our gratitude to him, is by serving our neighbours.

Assessment

For the situation ethicist (Fletcher maintains), love is the only ethical standard, and the only right action, in any situation, is the most loving one. Love is the first principle of situation ethics, and like any first principle it cannot be proved but can only be vindicated by its success in practice. But, how can the situationist be sure that he will always do the most loving thing? According to Fletcher, he must recognize that every situation is unique, and that circumstances alter cases. He must be calculating, in the positive sense. He must tease out every aspect of every situation, before he acts, so as to ensure that his action really is the most loving.

Fletcher does not dismiss established ethical principles out of hand. He believes that a situationist should approach every ethical decision with his community's ethical principles in mind. And he should treat them with respect for the light they shed on ethical decisions. However, he must not regard them as inviolable, and he must be prepared to modify them, or set them aside completely, if that is what love demands. As love is the only principle, subordinate principles, including even those in the Ten Commandments, however important, and whatever the extent to which experience has shown that following them produces the best outcome, cannot be treated as absolute. For in this particular situation applying a firmly established principle may not maximize love. Yes, in general, lying will not be the most loving thing to do; but it could be here and now. The same is true even of killing; and not only, as in Bonhoeffer's case, to rid the world of a mad and murderous megalomaniac, but even when it involves the mass slaughter caused by exploding a nuclear bomb.

We can agree with Fletcher that situations demanding ethical decisions may be too complex for the straightforward application of a general principle, such as 'do not lie', or 'do not steal'. Such situations require careful analysis and assessment, and it may be extremely difficult to decide just what is the right thing to do. However, while Fletcher emphasizes the importance of calculating each moral situation carefully, he does not, in the examples he gives, clearly explain or justify why a particular choice is the most loving. For example, it is possible to explain and justify President Truman's decision to drop atomic bombs on Hiroshima and Nagasaki, on the grounds that it was the most effective way to bring the war with Japan to an end; it was the best means of minimizing the loss of Allied soldiers' lives; and it also meant that the rest of the population of Japan was spared the trauma of a full-scale invasion of the Japanese mainland. However, Fletcher does not do so. He does not explain how and why this judgement was made, and precisely why it was, in his view, the most loving.

In places, he also seems to suggest that there may be many situations in which it would be right to set aside such fundamental moral principles as not killing or lying, when, particularly with the first, they are likely to be extremely rare. Further, despite what he says to the contrary, he gives the impression that it is relatively easy to determine all the morally relevant aspects of a situation and, by means of the so-called agapeic calculus, to determine all the consequences of an action. It fact, as Mill concedes in *Utilitarianism*, and Moore stresses in *Principia Ethica*, it may be extremely difficult to do so: which is why it is generally better to apply a well-tested principle rather than to try to calculate the consequences of modifying or suspending it.

We come back to the problem that applying the love ethic in actual situations is far from straightforward, and not only because of the difficulty of calculating consequences. For what is the most loving action in this or that situation? There is no objective criterion by which to decide that matter. It is likely to prove highly subjective, with each situationist judging the most loving action to be what fits in with his own moral preferences or prejudices, or even what suits his own self-interest. In practice, the most truly loving actions are likely to be those which apply well-established moral principles, and which, at the very least, embody the principle of non-maleficence.

So, was Fletcher naive? Did he overestimate the extent to which people would want to do the 'most loving thing'? If so, he was not alone among theologians and religious ethicists of the 1960s. In *Honest to God*, the then Bishop of Woolwich John Robinson, referring to earlier accounts by Fletcher of the 'new morality', wrote approvingly that it was:

> the only ethic for 'man come of age' . . . If we have the cour-
> age, it is something to be welcomed – as a challenge to
> Christian ethics to shake itself loose from the supports of
> supranaturalistic legalism . . . For nothing can of itself al-
> ways be labelled as 'wrong'. One cannot, for instance, start
> from the position 'sex relations before marriage' or 'divorce'
> are wrong or sinful in themselves. They may be in 99 cases
> or even 100 . . . but they are not intrinsically so, for the only
> intrinsic evil is lack of love. (pp. 117–18)

And we can appreciate just how naive this whole approach is when we read Robinson's account of how a young man might apply the situational approach to the issue of his desire to make love to his girlfriend:

> To the young man asking in his relations with a girl, 'Why
> shouldn't I?', it is relatively easy to say, 'Because it's wrong'
> or 'Because it's a sin' – and then to condemn him when
> he . . . takes no notice. It makes much greater demands to
> ask, and to answer, the question 'Do you love her?' . . . and
> then to help him to accept *for himself* the decision that, if he
> doesn't . . . his action is immoral, or, if he does, then he will
> respect her far too much to use her . . . (p. 119)

Well, perhaps. Or he may just be thankful that no one is lay-
ing down the law and telling him that he definitely should not

make love to his girlfriend, and decide that the 'most loving thing to do' is certainly to follow his instincts and do so. What 'man come of age' (which means people who no longer feel themselves bound by traditional, religious-based morality) need is not a vague injunction to 'do the most loving thing' but a universal principle which relates precisely to the ethical issue they are grappling with, such as: 'You should always treat others, and particularly your girlfriend, as ends-in-themselves, never merely as means, in this case to your own immediate gratification. So, you should only have sexual relations with her if you love her; if you intend to have a permanent relationship with her; and if you are sure that she really wants to have sexual relations with you. What you should both avoid at all costs is having unprotected sex, which could result in an unwanted child and the spread of sexually transmitted diseases.'

Richard Neuhaus is probably right when he says of Fletcher and situation ethics that it is:

> redolent with the confidence that almost everybody is pretty much like Joe Fletcher – fundamentally decent, ever so enlightened, eminently reasonable, and eager to do the right thing ... In his last years, Fletcher deplored the moral sleaze of a culture that acted on the doctrine that he championed: it's right if it's right for you. Neglecting the human will, Fletcher was blind to the human propensity for evil. Assuming that the Protestantism into which he was born had an inexhaustible supply of moral capital, Fletcher did not reckon with the consequences of bankruptcy.

Finally, what about the fact that, although Fletcher writes about Christian situation ethics, he renounced Christian belief, and became a secular humanist, not long after the book was published? Does this invalidate *Situation Ethics*, or any part of it? It certainly seems odd, and, as a secular humanist, Fletcher could no longer subscribe to those aspects of the book which invoke specifically Christian teachings, such as the belief that God is love, or the role of grace. However, Fletcher does make it clear that practising situation ethics and following the law of love do not require Christian commitment: the secularist can also relate his actions to the maximization of neighbour-centred love.

Some Key Quotations

General principles or maxims
The situationist enters into every decision-making situation fully armed with the ethical maxims of his community and its heritage, and he treats them with respect as illuminators of his problems. Just the same he is prepared in any situation to compromise them or set them aside *in the situation* if love seems better served by doing so. (p. 26)

The law of love
Christian *situation* ethics has only one norm or principle or law . . . always good and right, regardless of the circumstances. That is 'love' – the *agape* of the summary commandment to love God and the neighbor. (p. 30)

Love and reason
Situation ethics . . . calls upon us to keep law in a subservient place, so that *only* love and reason really count . . . (p. 31)

Every situation is unique
Situationists ask . . . if there ever are enough cases enough

alike to validate a law or to support anything more than a cautious generalization. (p. 32)

Love is the ultimate standard
Christianly speaking, as we shall see, the norm or measure by which any thought or action is to be judged a success or failure, i.e., right or wrong, is *love*. (p. 43)

The situationist never says 'never'
The situationist avoids words like 'never' and 'perfect' and 'complete' as he avoids the plague, as he avoids 'absolutely'. (pp. 43–4)

Relativizing the absolute
There must be an absolute or norm of some kind if there is to be any true relativity. This is the central fact in the normative relativism of a situation ethic . . . In *Christian* situationism the ultimate criterion is . . . 'agapeic love'. It relativizes the absolute, it does not absolutize the relative! (pp. 44–5)

No proof of the highest good
Any moral or value judgment in ethics, like a theologian's faith proposition, is a *decision* – not a conclusion . . . The hedonist cannot 'prove' that pleasure is the highest good, any more than the Christian can 'prove' his faith that *love* is! (p. 47)

God is love
The Christian does not understand God in terms of love; he understands love in terms of God as seen in Christ. (p. 49)

Persons determine values
There are no 'values' in the sense of inherent goods – value

is what *happens* to something when it happens to be useful to love working for the sake of persons. (p. 50)

Conscience

There *is* no conscience; 'conscience' is merely a word for our attempts to make decisions creatively, constructively, fittingly . . . the reason making moral judgments. (p. 53)

It all depends on the situation

The rightness of an act . . . nearly always and perhaps always, depends on the way in which the act is related to circumstances . . . (p. 59)

Loving is doing

Love is the only universal. But love is not something we *have* or *are*, it is something we *do*. Our task is to act so that more good (i.e., loving-kindness) will occur than any possible alternatives; we are to be 'optimific', to seek an optimum of loving-kindness. (pp. 60–1)

Lying can be loving

If a lie is told unlovingly it is wrong, evil; if it is told in love it is good, right. (p. 65)

Jesus was a situationist

Christian situation ethics reduces law from a statutory system of rules to the love canon alone. For this reason, Jesus was ready without hesitation to ignore the obligations of Sabbath observance, to do forbidden work on the seventh day. (p. 69)

The Bible is not a rules book

Either cheap melancholy or utter frustration will follow if we turn the Bible into a rules book, forgetting that an editorial collection of scattered sayings, such as the Sermon on the Mount, offers us at the most some paradigms or suggestions. (p. 77)

The new morality
In its very marrow Christian ethics is a situation ethic. The new morality, the emerging contemporary Christian conscience, separates Christian conduct from rigid creeds and rigid codes. (p. 77)

The nature of *agape* love
Agape is giving love – non-reciprocal, neighbor-regarding – 'neighbor' meaning 'everybody,' even an enemy . . . (p. 79)

Ethical rules are no safeguard against selfish motives
If it is supposed that the situational method of moral decision-making is too open to a conscious or unconscious rationalizing of selfish and evasive motives, we need only to remember that self-deceit and excuse-making can exploit *law* too for its own purposes . . . Our real motives can hide as effectively behind rules as behind free contextual choices. (p. 85)

Love plus careful calculation equals justice
Prudence, careful calculation, gives love the care-fulness it needs; with proper care, love does more than take justice into account, it *becomes* justice. (p. 88)

Human rights are validated by love
It is often said that what is 'due' to the neighbor is giving him his 'rights'. But . . . for situation ethics the same reasoning obtains. You have a right to anything that is loving; you have

no right to anything that is unloving. All alleged rights and duties are as contingent and relative as all values. The right to religious freedom, free speech, public assembly, private property, sexual liberty, life itself, the vote – *all* are validated only by love. (p. 95)

The agapeic calculus
. . . the hedonistic calculus becomes the agapeic calculus, the greatest amount of neighbor welfare for the largest number of neighbors possible. (p. 95)

Everyone is our neighbour
The radical obligation of the Christian ethic is to love not only the stranger-neighbor and the acquaintance-neighbor but even the enemy-neighbor . . . (p. 107)

Calculation is not cruel
Moral choices need intelligence as much as they need concern, sound information as well as good disposition. (p. 114)

Ends and means
And *therefore* what is sometimes good may at other times be evil, and what is sometimes wrong may sometimes be right when it serves a good enough end – *depending on the situation.* (p. 123)

An antisituational gambit
The 'generalization argument' (What would happen if everybody did it?) is actually one of the maneuvers used to discredit personal responsibility and leave law in control. It is a fundamentally antisituational gambit. (p. 131)

On sexual morality
... if people do not believe it is wrong to have sex relations outside marriage, it isn't, unless they hurt themselves, their partners, or others. (p. 140)

Making ethical decisions situationally, not prescriptively
Legal rights are subordinate, and so are legal prohibitions ... For although law may sometimes be the matter of love, there are other times when law denies love and destroys it. The core difference, however, is that *loves decisions are made situationally, not prescriptively.* (pp. 144–5)

Suggestions for Further Reading

Joseph Fletcher, *Morals and Medicine*, Princeton, NJ: Princeton University Press, 1954.

Joseph Fletcher, *Memoirs of an Ex-Radical*, Louisville, KY: Westminster John Knox, 1993.

Joseph Fletcher, *Moral Responsibility: Situation Ethics at Work*, Louisville, KY: Westminster John Knox, 1967.

Joseph Fletcher, *Situation Ethics*, London: SCM Press, 1966.

Joseph Fletcher, *The Ethics of Genetic Control: Ending Reproductive Roulette*, Amherst, NY: Prometheus Books, 1988.

Joseph Fletcher and Spencer Miller, *The Church and Industry*, New York, Longmans, Green and Co., 1930.

Joseph Fletcher, *William Temple, Twentieth Century Christian*, New York: Seabury, 1963.

Harvey Cox (ed.) and Joseph Fletcher, *The Situation Ethics Debate*, Louisville, KY: Westminster Press, 1968.

R. M. Hare, 'Universal Prescriptivism', in P. Singer (ed.), *A Companion to Ethics*, London: Blackwell, 1991.

W. D. Hudson, *Modern Moral Philosophy*, London: Macmillan, 1970 (Chapter 5).

David Hume, *A Treatise of Human Nature*, Mineola, NY: Dover Publications, 2003.

John Stuart Mill, *Utilitarianism*, ed. G. Sher, second edition, Indianapolis/Cambridge: Hackett Publishing Company, 2001.

G. E. Moore, *Principia Ethica*, ed. T. Baldwin, revised edition, Cambridge: Cambridge University Press, 1993.

R. Neuhaus, 'All too human', *National Review*, December, 1991. Online at http://findarticles.com.

J. A. T. Robinson, *Honest to God*, London: SCM Press, 1963 (Chapter 6).

P. Vardy and P. Grosch, *The Puzzle of Ethics*, revised edition, London: HarperCollins, 1999 (Chapter 10).

Detailed Summary of Joseph Fletcher's
Situation Ethics: The New Morality

Foreword (pp. 11–16)

Some critics have described **e. e. cummings'** six *'nonlectures* on poetry' at Harvard as 'six lectures on nonpoetry' and, while **Bishop John Robinson** has taken the opposite view of my ethical theory, others have said that it is a 'non-Christian system of non-ethics' (p. 11). Below, the reader will find, in keeping with Jesus' ethic, 'a method, but no system'; there can be no 'system of Christian ethics', if it is to be 'true to its nature' (pp. 11–12). Nor is it exactly a **'new morality'**, although it departs from 'the conventional wisdom' (pp. 12–13). I can illustrate the approach by the story of a St Louis 'cab driver', who explained to a friend of mine his intention not to follow his family's tradition of voting Republican thus: 'there are times when a man has to push his principles aside and do the right thing' (p. 13). He is 'this book's hero' (p. 13).

Christian situationism is both **'personalistic** and **contextual'**; by the latter, I mean 'tailored to fit objective circumstances' (p. 14). Some say that I do not make it very Christian, as I make insufficient reference to the 'theological framework' (p. 15). However, there is plenty of stress on 'the **normative** ideal of "love"' (p. 15). But, given its ambiguity, should we use this word as it stands or just use the 'word *agape*' or '**C-love**', to make what we are talking about absolutely unambiguous (p. 15). I prefer not to, as 'love' is 'too rich, with too much important and legitimate meaning' to cast it aside (p. 15).

I Three Approaches (pp. 17–39)

There are three ways of 'making moral decisions', all of which have featured in the '**history of Western morals**': '**legalistic**', '**antinomian**' and '**situational**' (p. 17). Is it the case that, for example, sex outside marriage is always 'inherently evil' or can it sometimes be a 'good thing' (p. 18)? Are all of us 'immoral and ethically weak' (p. 18)?

APPROACHES TO DECISION-MAKING (pp. 18–31)
1 Legalism (pp. 18–22)

This approach is found in the major western 'religious traditions' of Judaism, Roman Catholicism and Protestantism, and involves a set of fixed 'rules and regulations' that can be looked up in a book, such as the Bible, and which prescribe certain actions (p. 18). At the same time, reflecting the complexity of life, an 'elaborate system of exceptions' develops, giving rise to 'hairsplitting' (pp. 18–9). Thus, in Roman Catholicism there is an 'ingenious **moral theology**', which, prompted by 'love of persons', uses '**casuistry**' to escape its own rigid '"laws" of right' (p. 19). Protestantism's laws have been less 'intricate', but its 'puritanical' emphasis on 'moral rules' shows that it is no longer conscious of life's 'headaches and heartbreaks' (pp. 19–20). Worse still, absence of casuistry may mean using law sadistically 'to hurt people', not help them (p. 20). Look at the way homosexuals are still treated in some places, even if they are 'consenting adults' (p. 20). A Christian **'situation ethicist'** endorses **Bertrand Russell**'s implied criticism that Christians judge 'an adulterer' more severely than a corrupt politician, even though the latter causes more harm, and rejects **Cardinal Newman**'s view that it would be better for 'sun and moon' to fall from heaven than for 'one soul' to commit a 'single venial sin' (p. 20).

A woman whose teenage daughter had given birth to three 'unwanted, neglected babies' urged her to use contraception (pp. 20–1). Secular law and **'legalistic puritanism'** combined to convict and sentence her (p. 21). Christian legalism has taken two forms. With Roman Catholic moralists, it has been a matter of **'legalistic** *reason*', based on nature or **natural law**. They have applied human reason to the 'facts of nature' and human experience, and have claimed the outcome as **'valid "natural" moral laws'** (p. 21). Protestants have been equally 'legalistic', but their **'moral law'** is based on interpretation of **biblical revelation** (p. 21).

2 Antinomianism (pp. 22–5)

With this 'polar opposite', one approaches moral decision-making situations without any 'principles or maxims whatsoever'; any solution must be found in the *'there and then'* (p. 22). **St Paul** had to do battle with it, as he does, for example, in **1 Corinthians 6.12–20**; and it also crops up as **libertinism**: the view that, as a result of **'grace', the 'new life in Christ and salvation by faith'**, Christians need no longer be bound by laws (p. 22). The **Gnostics** claimed to have 'special knowledge', such that they would always *'know* what was right' (pp. 22–3). They so wholeheartedly rejected moral rules that their 'moral decisions' were spontaneous, 'random' and 'literally unprincipled', even to the extent of ignoring 'love as it has been shown in Christ' (p. 23). Some professed to have a special 'radarlike "faculty"', rather like the **'intuition theory or faculty theory of conscience'** (pp. 23–4). A modern version of antinomianism is found in the 'ethics of **existentialism'** (p. 24). Jean-Paul **Sartre** denies that there are 'any *generally* valid principles at all', never mind 'universal *laws*' (p. 25). He contends that, as life has no 'fabric or web', there is no justification for formulating 'moral principles *or* laws': 'every situation has only its particularity!' (p. 25).

3 Situationism (pp. 26–31)

This occupies the middle ground. The situationist approaches every 'decision-making situation' with a respectful awareness of his community's 'ethical maxims', which he believes can shed light on his problem (p. 26). However, he is not tied hand and foot by them; he will modify or jettison them if, in that situation, 'love seems better served by doing so' (p. 26). He goes so far with both natural law, as he accepts 'reason as the instrument of moral judgment', and 'Scriptural law', as he accepts that revelation has provided the only **moral norm** that cannot be compromised: 'to **love God in the neighbor'** (p. 26).

The situationist's moral decisions are **'hypothetical'**, not **'categorical'**, as the only 'categorically good' commandment is to love (p. 26). As **Brunner** says, the basis of the **'Divine Command'** remains the same, but the 'content varies' (p. 27). Although we can derive general principles to guide our conduct from the **'one and only universal law'**, which Christians call *'agape'*, we cannot bind ourselves by 'laws or rules', as they might prevent loving behaviour (p. 27). **William Temple** said that what acts are right may depend on the situation, and the situationist believes that what we are obliged to do is 'relative *to* the situation' (p. 27). It is not always right to tell the truth, for example, if a murderer wants to know where his potential victim is. There is a variety of labels for this approach to ethics, such as '**situationism, contextualism**' and '**circumstantialism**' (p. 29). Its core is a 'healthy and primary awareness that "circumstances alter cases"', and that, in moral decisions, '**situational variables**' have to be considered just as much as general principles (p. 29).

Christian situation ethics is 'case-focused and concrete' (p. 29). It operates by just one 'binding' norm, which is always right: '"love" – the *agape* of the summary commandment to love God and the neighbor', and it attempts to 'relate love to a world of relativities' (pp. 30–1). The highest good will be different in non-Christian situation ethics, such as '**self-realization** in the ethics of **Aristotle**' (p. 31).

PRINCIPLES, YES, BUT NOT RULES (pp. 31–7)

In accordance with his '**principled relativism**', the situationist holds that '*only* love and reason really count' (p. 31). He asks whether enough cases are sufficiently alike to 'validate a law or to support anything more than a cautious generalization' (p. 32). **Dietrich Bonhoeffer** pointed out that the question of what is good is 'posed and is decided' in each 'unique and transient situation'; and he himself is the 'Christian ethicist', executed for attempting to kill '**Adolf Hitler** – so far did he go as a situationist' (p. 33). Of course, the 'basic legalism of classical Christian ethics' will oppose the 'situational **love ethic**' by all possible means; but this does not deflect the situationist from averring that there is just one moral principle: 'love, without any prefabricated recipes for what it means in practice'; and that any other so-called moral principles must be treated as 'relative to particular, concrete situations' (p. 36).

ABORTION: A SITUATION (pp. 37–9)

In 1962, an unmarried girl with severe '**schizophrenic psychosis**' was raped by a fellow patient in a state mental hospital (p. 37). Her father asked for an immediate **abortion** to terminate the 'unwanted pregnancy' (p. 37). It was refused, on the grounds that the law permitted only '**therapeutic' abortions**, where the mother's life was at risk (p. 37). Here, the moral legalist would resist abortion on the grounds that 'killing is absolutely wrong', while the **Catholic moral theologian** would go further, insisting that there could be no 'exceptions' (pp. 37–8). The situationist, judging by the norm of the 'Christian commandment to love the neighbor', would, in this case, urge abortion, 'for the sake of the patient's physical and mental health', not merely to save her life, and because 'no *unwanted and unintended* baby' should be born (p. 39). Further, he would argue that it is '*not* killing because there is **no person or human life in an embryo at an early stage of pregnancy**' (p. 39).

II Some Presuppositions (pp. 40–56)

There are some 'preliminary matters' to deal with, before going on to explore 'how love works in ethical decision-making' (p. 40).

FOUR WORKING PRINCIPLES *(pp. 40–52)*
1 *Pragmatism (pp. 40–3)*

One inspiration for this book is '**American** *pragmatism*', for just as he now understands the central role of the 'situational' in the quest for 'the right and the good', this writer also appreciates that philosophy cannot bridge the 'gap between doubt and faith' (p. 41). Bonhoeffer and **Kierkegaard** were right to reject '**metaphysics**' and **philosophical 'systems'** (p. 41). American pragmatism and '**British empiricism**' have always focused on what is true; and truth and goodness are not 'separable' (p. 41). As **William James** put it, the true and the good are the 'expedient' in how we think and behave; in other words, the good and the true are 'whatever works' (pp. 41–2).

Of course, pragmatism itself does not provide the 'norms' we require to assess the 'success' it demands: to be correct or right, something must work, but 'to what end' (p. 42)? The key question here is that of 'value': what do we choose as our '*summum bonum*' or highest good (p. 43)? From the Christian standpoint, the norm by which we evaluate the 'success or failure', that is, the rightness or wrongness, of any action is '*love*' (p. 43).

2 *Relativism (pp. 43–6)*

Our approach to ethics is also '*relativistic*'; we can say that it is strategically pragmatic and tactically 'relativistic' (p. 43). A situationist shuns such words as 'never', 'perfect', 'complete' and 'absolutely' (pp. 43–4). There is a paradox at the heart of situation ethics, which is that there must be 'an absolute' standard for there to be 'any true relativity': our actions are right to the extent that they measure up to the 'ultimate criterion' of '**agapeic love**', which 'relativizes the absolute' but does not 'absolutize the relative' (pp. 44–5). We are always commanded to act lovingly, but there are no binding principles, no absolute rules, as to how we should do so: the right thing for us to do in a particular situation depends on 'our own *responsible* estimate' of that situation (p. 45). **Paul Tillich** has written that the 'truth of **ethical relativism**' lies in the fact that moral laws are incapable of providing commands which are 'unambiguous' in their 'general form' and 'concrete applications' (p. 46). It is essential that 'contemporary Christians' do not underplay this 'relativism', which has been part of 'Christian ethics' ever since Jesus denounced the '**Pharisees' principle of statutory morality**', and Paul appealed to '**grace and freedom**' (p. 46).

3 *Positivism (pp. 46–50)*

Positivism, that is, '**theological positivism**', in which '**faith propositions' are affirmed 'voluntaristically**', is also important (p. 47). In Christian ethics, we do not begin by reasoning to, or finding reasons for, faith in God: we start with faith in God, and then reason out 'what obedience to his commandment to love requires in any situation' (p. 47). And this is no different from what happens in any ethical system, where the choice of the highest good is, like the 'theologian's faith proposition', a *'decision* – not a conclusion' (p. 47). A **utilitarian** such as **John Stuart Mill** could not prove that pleasure/happiness is the highest good, any more than a Christian can prove 'his faith that *love* is' (p. 47). Reason can 'note facts' and 'infer relations', but it 'cannot find values (goodness)' (p. 48). Values are chosen and 'normative standards' adopted in a way that is just as '**arbitrary and absurd as the leap of faith**' (p. 48). As

David Hume explained, there is **no logical bridge from 'facts to values, from isness to oughtness'**: our moral choices may be 'vindicated', but cannot be 'validated' (p. 49).

In Christian ethics, love or *'agape'* is established as the '**axiomatic value**' by the faith affirmation that '**God is love**', from which we can infer that 'love is the highest good' (p. 49). As Christians, we do not 'understand God in terms of love', but 'love in terms of God as seen in Christ' (p. 49). Paul's statement about '**faith working through love**' is the 'essence' of Christian ethics (p. 49).

4 Personalism (pp. 50–2)

Situation ethics puts people, not things, at 'the center of concern': obligations are to persons, so situationists are *'personalistic'* (p. 50). Indeed, there are no values, in the sense of things that are inherently good, for things become valuable when they are 'useful to love working for the sake of persons' (p. 50). But this is not 'individualistic' (p. 50). Just as good derives from people's needs, so people 'derive from society', and only free persons, capable of being responsible selves, can sustain relationships and undertake obligations (pp. 50–1). There is also a theological aspect to the personalism of Christian ethics, as God is 'personal' and has '**created men in his own image**' (p. 51). Thus, **Kant**'s second formulation of the **categorical imperative** holds true, and we must **treat persons always as ends, never merely as means** (p. 51).

In fact, things are to be used; and it is people who are to be loved, so it is 'immoral' when the reverse is the case (p. 51). 'Loving actions are the *only* conduct permissible', and it is not non-believers who invite '"damnation" but the unloving' (pp. 51–2).

Situation ethics involves making decisions, not '"looking them up" in a manual of prefab rules' (p. 52). Its concern is not with what is good, but with how to do it and for whom: not with 'what *is* love' but with 'how to *do* the most loving thing possible in the situation' (p. 52).

CONSCIENCE *(pp. 52–6)*

Situation ethics' interest in **'conscience (moral consciousness)' is 'as a function'**, **not 'a faculty'**, taking account of it only when it is 'working, practicing, deciding' (pp. 52–3). We believe that there is no such entity as a conscience: the term is simply a way of referring to our efforts to make decisions 'creatively, constructively, fittingly'; it is our reason 'making moral judgments' (p. 53). Again, our concern is with **'antecedent rather than consequent conscience'**: with making future moral judgements, not passing judgement on actions performed previously (p. 54). Paul was right to describe conscience as a '*director* of human decisions', not a 'reviewer' (p. 54).

Situation ethics, with its **'pragmatic-empirical temper'**, applies itself to specific situations, seeking, on the basis of experience, to work out general and tentative ideas about how to deal with them (p. 55). It studies each case in all its **'contextual particularity**, deferring in fear and trembling only to the rule of love', and keeping ethical principles sternly in their place: they are **'advisers without veto power!'** (p. 55). Situation ethicists affirm only one general principle: to 'love God through the neighbor' (p. 55). All other principles are '*maxims*, **never rules'** (p. 55).

III Love Only Is Always Good (pp. 57–68)

Is a thing's worthiness or unworthiness 'inherent *in* it', or is it *'relative* to other things' (p. 57)?

NOMINAL GOOD (pp. 57–60)

For God, what is 'valuable' is 'whatever suits his (love's) needs and purposes', and, at the level of human value judgements, situation ethics is '**nominalistic**' in the same way (pp. 57–8). There are no (absolute) 'values', only material and non-material things, which persons happen to value; and this is the '**personalist view**' (p. 58). In Christian situation ethics, nothing has value 'in and of itself', but derives its value, or lack of it, from the fact that it happens to help or harm persons (p. 59). Indeed, 'Persons – God, self, neighbor', are the 'subjects and the objects of value', as they determine a thing's, or an action's, value, 'for some person's sake' (p. 59). An action which is right in one situation, such as lending money to a father who needs it to feed his hungry family, may be wrong in another: for example, if the father is 'known to be a compulsive gambler or alcoholic' (p. 59). Thus, an act's rightness invariably depends on how it is 'related to circumstances' (p. 59).

LOVE IS A PREDICATE (pp. 60–4)

Christian situation ethics holds firmly that: '*Value, worth, ethical quality, goodness or badness, right or wrong – these things are only predicates, they are not properties*' (p. 60). We must be clear that love is not a substance but a principle which expresses 'what type of real actions Christians are to call good' (p. 60).

It is the only universal value, but it is not 'something we *have* or *are*', but 'something we *do*' (pp. 60–1). We must so act as to produce more good, that is, 'loving-kindness', than would be produced by any alternative action (p. 61). Our disposition must be '**optimific**', seeking an 'optimum of loving-kindness' (p. 61). It is an 'attitude, a disposition, a leaning, a preference, a purpose' (p. 61).

Being loving is a 'way of relating to persons, and of using things' (p. 61). As **H. R. Niebuhr** explains, it is not commanded 'for its own sake', but for that of others (p. 61). It is not a '**virtue**', but the sole '*regulative principle* of Christian ethics' (p. 61).

When we understand love 'situationally', as a predicate, not a property, we can appreciate that 'Jesus' going to the cross was *his* role and vocation in *his* situation with *his* obligation as the Son of God' (pp. 61–2). We cannot join **Reinhold Niebuhr** in talking of the '**impossibility**' **of love**, but we agree with him about its '*relativity*' (p. 62). Love does not say, '*Be* like me', but '*Do* what you can where you are' (p. 62). Love is only substantive in God, because 'God *is* love' (p. 62). We, however, are finite, and 'only *do* love', trying, in obedience, to 'obey love's command to be like God, to imitate him', and 'to love the neighbor' (pp. 62–3). And we must remember that God is 'not reason but love', employing the former merely as his love's 'instrument'; and this is 'the **theology of situation ethics**' (p. 63).

Love's opposite is not 'hate but indifference'; the first at least 'treats the neighbor as a *thou*', whereas the second makes of him 'an *it*, a thing' (p. 63). The one thing worse than evil itself is indifference to it. We must keep in mind the New Testament injunction to 'love people, not principles' (p. 64). Kant's **second maxim**, to treat people always as ends, and never merely as means, is 'strictly parallel to the New Testament's "law of love"', and his contention that a 'good will' is the 'only really good thing' is 'what the New Testament means by *agape* or "love"' (p. 64). And this goes logically with his view that what is 'benevolent is right; whatever is malevolent or indifferent is wrong' (p. 64).

ONLY EXTRINSIC (pp. 64–8)

The situation ethics perspective is opposed to all '"**intrinsical-ist" ethics**', the view that there are 'objectively valid' laws and maxims (p. 64). For, if a lie is told 'unlovingly' it is wrong, but if it is told lovingly it is right (p. 65). **Kant's 'legalism'** produced a universal ethical principle, that lying is always wrong; but what if you have to lie to keep a 'promised secret' (p. 65)? Then, you are right to 'follow love's lead', for right and wrong, good and bad, are what happen to the things we say and do, irrespective of whether we tell the truth or not: it all depends on 'how much love is served in the situation' (p. 65).

The idea that value, that is, good or evil, is a property which can be found in our actions is the '**backbone of all legalism**' (p. 66). The **extrinsicalism of situation ethics** joins battle with the '**unlovingness of law-bound conscience**', which '**reifies good and evil**' and treats 'value as if it were a thing-in-itself', not a 'function of human decisions' (p. 67). Here is our '**norma-tive relativism**', which dismisses 'legalism and **dogmatism**' (p. 67). For '**classical moralists**', suicide and lying are always wrong, irrespective of circumstances, despite the fact that in a particular situation such actions may be justified by 'lov-ing concern' (p. 67). No law or principle of value is good in itself, not even 'life or truth or **chastity** or property or mar-riage': '*Only one thing is intrinsically good, namely, love: nothing else at all*' (p. 68).

IV Love Is the Only Norm (pp. 69–86)

Love is a '**monolithic and jealous standard, a univalent norm**', which ousts 'lesser goods' (p. 69). Christian situation ethics transforms morality from a '**statutory system of rules**' to the '**love canon alone**' (p. 69). This is why Jesus unhesitatingly ignored the **rules of 'Sabbath observance**', and did 'forbidden work' on it (p. 69).

LOVE REPLACES LAW (pp. 69–71)

Jesus and Paul substituted the 'living principle of *agape*' for the '**precepts of Torah**', thus redeeming moral laws from the 'letter that kills', and infusing into it the 'spirit that gives it life' (p. 69). The situationist's response to the claim that love requires us to abide by the law is that we are prepared to do so, but only on condition that 'they serve love' (p. 71). Often, 'love and law' conflict: they cannot be partners, and 'love only employs law when it seems worthwhile' (p. 71).

TABLETS OF STONE (pp. 71–5)

What about the **Ten Commandments**? Surely, we cannot break these? But, this is not so. Take the first: 'I am the Lord your God, you shall have no other gods before me' (p. 71). This is a tautology, not a true commandment: it says only that if we 'have faith in one God', we will not have faith in another (p. 71). And 'under persecution' we could break it, for 'love's sake' (p. 72). The same is true of the second and third: not making a graven image or taking God's name in vain. As for keeping the sabbath day, how can we do so in our 'interdependent society', when goods have to be produced at the weekend (p. 73)? The final six, for 'filial piety' and against killing, adultery, stealing, false witness and covetousness, are more ethical, but situation ethics maintains that on occasions our duty is to break '*any or all of them*' (p. 74). We must exchange the 'legalist's love of law' for the 'law of love' (p. 74).

NEITHER NATURE NOR SCRIPTURE (pp. 75–7)

Inevitably, every form of religious legalism, whether of the 'Catholic natural law' or of the 'Protestant Scriptural law' variety, is rejected (p. 75). To the advocates of the former, we say that there are no universal ethical principles which all human beings, at all times, have subscribed to. The ethical precepts, which all human beings can accept are 'platitudes', like 'do the good and avoid the evil' or 'to each according to his due' (p. 76). What is good, and the 'when and how' of it, has been and always will be 'widely debated', as applied to 'concrete cases' (p. 76). To the advocates of the latter, we say that only frustration will result from turning the 'Bible into a rules book', and forgetting that a **'collection of scattered sayings'**, like the **Sermon on the Mount**, offers not a list of rules but a set of 'suggestions' (p. 77).

LOVE HAS NO EQUALS (pp. 77–81)

In its essence, 'Christian ethics is a situation ethic' (p. 77). This 'new morality' distinguishes 'Christian conduct from rigid creeds and rigid codes' (p. 77). Love is not 'one principle among equals', but what **Augustine** makes it: the **'source principle'** (p. 78). And he was right to reduce the 'whole Christian ethic' to the 'single maxim': 'Love with care and *then* what you will, do' (p. 79). However, Christian love is not desire. '*Agape* is giving love' which is '**non-reciprocal**' and '**neighbor-regarding**', and our 'neighbor' includes everybody, even our enemies (p. 79). It must be distinguished from '**friendship love (*philia*)**' and '**romantic love (*eros*)**', both of which are 'selective and exclusive' (p. 79). As situation ethicists, by making love our standard or norm we find ourselves to be both free and responsible. We do not need to pretend that we should follow standards, such as '"**Christian" sex relations (marital monopoly)**', which are not our own (p. 80).

OBJECTIONS (pp. 81–6)

It is often objected that situation ethics requires more 'critical intelligence', 'factual information' and 'self-starting commitment to righteousness' than the majority possesses; that it disregards the 'reality of human sin', and fails to appreciate the limitations of 'human reason' (p. 81). Well, the situationist, particularly the Christian one, does need to be 'mature' and 'responsible' (p. 82). There is an '**Anglo-American principle**' **of minding your own business**, and the law limits our obligation to what we do, not what we should have done (p. 82). This is the 'prudence of self-centredness and indifference', which stands in sharp contrast to the '**aggressive, questing prudence of *agape***' (p. 82).

But it is 'cheap legalism' to hide behind the letter of the law in order to evade the 'higher demands of its spirit' (p. 83). Further, absolute 'negatives' and 'affirmatives' falsify 'complex realities' (p. 83). **Albert Schweitzer** was right to hold that 'good conscience' is the devil's invention (p. 83). Take '**classical pacifism**', which regards any violence as always wrong, irrespective of the situation (p. 83). This is 'legalism': it makes the pacifist 'safe ethically', because he never has to face the problem of having to make decisions of a certain kind (pp. 83–4). If, as the situationist believes, our opinions are only as good as our facts, it is essential that we know 'what's what when we act' (p. 84). The situationist does not allow 'prefabricated decisions' to be imposed on 'free people in living situations' (pp. 84–5).

To the charge that the situational approach is too liable to 'conscious or unconscious rationalizing of selfish and evasive motives', our response is that 'self-deceit and excuse-making' can manipulate moral laws for their own purposes as well: 'real motives' can be as easily concealed behind rules as '**free contextual choices**' (p. 85).

V Love and Justice Are the Same (pp. 87–102)

Almost every problem that involves a 'perplexed conscience', as opposed to a 'doubtful' one, can be reduced to the 'tension between love and justice' (p. 87).

LOVE IS CAREFUL (pp. 87–9)

'*Christian* love' and '*Christian* prudence' are the same thing: they both reach out to others (pp. 87–8). Of course, 'self-centered' love and 'prudence' are quite different (p. 88). The point is that prudence, that is, 'careful calculation', gives to love necessary 'care-fulness' (p. 88) So, with 'proper care' love not only takes justice into account but '*becomes* justice' (p. 88). If our definition of love is 'giving to others what is their due', we must redefine it in Christian terms: for what is due to our neighbours is '*only* love' (pp. 88–9). So, 'love is justice, justice is love' (p. 89).

Further, if justice means giving each person 'his due', how are we to calculate its distribution 'among so many'? For agapeic love is not a 'one-to-one affair', and 'uses a shotgun, not a rifle' (p. 89). Life is 'complex', and we have a 'web of duties', involving many people (p. 89). So, in order to be '**omnified**', love is forced to be 'calculating, careful, prudent, distributive', to take everything into account, and to be 'optimific' (p. 89).

WRONGFUL SEPARATION (pp. 89–92)

Justice is love's 'many-sidedness', for we are not concerned with giving love to only one other person; and sometimes the situation is extremely complex (p. 89). Love's 'simplest complication' is what we call '"commutative" justice', or 'one-to-one obligation', as when we buy and sell things, or make contracts (pp. 89–90). More challenging is 'distributive' or 'many-to-one' justice, as when a community shares out assets among its citizens, for example through 'retirement benefits': how much does love decree that each should receive (p. 90)? Equally complex is 'contributive' or 'one-to-many' justice, as when we pay our taxes: what should each individual pay (p. 90)?

Humbly, we must point out that 'Christian ethics' needs to modify Scripture: by adding an '"s" to "neighbor" in that distillation of the law' (p. 91). We must ensure that *agape* is not 'sentimentalized and individualized', by being reduced to 'one-to-one' (p. 91). This is how we can avoid the '**over-simplifying Tolstoyan**' **idea** that love is blind, 'never calculates', and is concerned only with the 'one-to-one *immediate* neighbor', who happens to be 'right there under your nose' (p. 91).

A PROPOSED REUNION (pp. 92–5)

The point to be stressed is that it is only a 'misdirected conscience' which has to contend with the 'justice *versus* love' problem (p. 92). Different schools of Christian ethics have 'related love and justice' in different ways: as 'love *versus* justice (opposites), love *or* justice (alternatives)', or 'love *and* justice (complements)' (p. 93). The Christian situationist says: 'love *is* justice', or 'justice loves', and 'to be just is to be loving' (p. 93). Reinhold Niebuhr, of course, made them alternatives, with love 'transcendent and impossible', and justice 'relative and possible'; but, instead of agreeing with Niebuhr, we should affirm that 'love is maximum justice and justice is optimum love' (p. 93). For Emil Brunner and William Temple, love governs **'interpersonal' relationships**, while justice applies to **'intergroup' relations** (p. 93). According to Roman Catholic moralists, love is a 'supernatural' virtue, and justice a 'natural' one: we are obliged to be just in our actions, but 'only *may* be loving' (pp. 93–4). But, justice is simply 'love working out its problems' (p. 95).

A common claim is that what is 'due' to our neighbour is to give him his 'rights' (p. 95). The situationist's response is that what the neighbour is entitled to is 'anything that is loving' and nothing that is 'unloving' (p. 95). Rights and duties, including such fundamental ones as the 'right to religious freedom, free speech, public assembly, private property, sexual liberty, life itself, the vote', are, like all values, 'contingent and relative': '*all* are validated only by love' (p. 95).

LOVE USING ITS HEAD (pp. 95–9)

Justice, then, is love when it has to cope with situations that require 'distribution' (p. 95). And this makes it clear that, in its search for a 'social policy', the 'love ethic' must ally itself with the **consequentialist** or **teleological** ethic of 'utilitarianism' (p. 95). From **Bentham** and Mill, it must adopt the '**strategic principle of "the greatest good of the greatest number"**', substituting *agape* for their '**pleasure principle**' (p. 95). Their '**hedonistic calculus**' becomes the '**agapeic calculus**', designed to calculate the greatest quantity of 'neighbor welfare for the largest number of neighbors possible' (p. 95). The Christian situationist's happiness consists of doing God's will, as expressed in '**Jesus' Summary**', and to pursue his own happiness, by promoting 'his neighbors' good on the widest possible scale' (p. 96). While situation ethics, which is concerned to realize or maximize good, has more in common with consequentialist than **deontological ethics**, it can also be understood in terms of the latter. Deontological ethics is *'duty* ethics', and is concerned with doing what is right, rather than promoting 'the good' (p. 96). As situationists, our duty is to maximize love 'in every situation' (p. 96).

Love does not allow us to solve problems at 'the expense of innocent third parties', for our neighbours are *'all* our neighbors' (p. 97). However, we must not allow sentimentality, or wrong-headed ideas about what love involves, to prevent us taking tough decisions. A doctor who gives the last available 'unit of blood plasma' to a mother of three in preference to an 'old skid row drunk' does not disregard love's equal 'concern for all neighbors' (pp. 97–8). He (and we) have to exercise our judgement, in order to apply love appropriately to specific situations. Love is 'responsible, thoughtful, careful', and requires us to examine each situation carefully, and calculate the outcomes of our choices, according to the amount of love they will produce (p. 98). Thus it was that on a 'vast scale of "agapeic calculus"' **President Truman** took the decision to drop '**A-bombs on Hiroshima and Nagasaki**' (p. 98).

ADDENDUM (pp. 99–102)

Situationists accept that 'law and order' are both necessary and good: 'wherever and whenever they promote the best interests of love' (p. 100). Sometimes, situation ethics welcomes 'law for love's sake': it all depends on the situation (p. 100). Thus, situation ethics does not endorse anarchy, for in society order is necessary, as well as love. But, again, judgement is essential. Justice must be 'understood agapeically', and laws may be right or wrong (p. 100). Our moral obligation is to be 'situational', and, for love's sake, we may need to disobey a law: our duty may be to obey the law, or not, which is determined by whether or not it serves our 'basic principle' of love (p. 101).

VI Love Is Not Liking (pp. 103–19)

Christian love is a 'matter of attitude', not feeling (p. 103).

NEVER SENTIMENTALIZE LOVE (pp. 103–7)

We must understand how it works. For example, a young, unmarried Christian couple may decide to have a sexual relationship, but their just liking each other would not make it right: there must be 'loving concern' for each other (p. 104). **C. H. Dodd** has described *agape* as 'primarily an **active determination of the will**', not 'an emotion or affection' (p. 105). So, unlike a feeling, it can be 'commanded' (p. 105). Those who mistakenly believe that 'true love' is an emotion will regard 'hate' as its opposite; in fact, it is 'indifference' (p. 105).

To be as precise as possible, Christian love is '**benevolence**' or goodwill (p. 105). *Agape* embraces our neighbours, not really for our own or even their sakes, but for God's. No, we are not, as Christians, called upon to like everybody; and this could not be ordered. But, *agape*, '*practical* love', can be (p. 106). We can be commanded to practise towards others such virtues, or '**dispositions of the will**', as 'kindness, generosity, mercy, patience, concern, righteous indignation, high resolve' (p. 106). These are the kind of virtues that Paul lists as '**fruits of the Spirit**' in Galatians (p. 107).

THE NEIGHBOUR IS ANYBODY (pp. 107–10)

As we see from **Matthew 5.43–48**, our obligation, as Christians, is to love not only the '**stranger-neighbor**' and the '**acquaintance-neighbor**', but even the '**enemy-neighbor**', in the same way that we love the '**friend-neighbor**' (p. 107). Christian love is not reciprocal or mutual; it does not expect any 'return of concern', although it hopes for it (p. 108). When the '**editor-compiler of Matthew's Sermon on the Mount**' concluded his section on love's 'universality and all-inclusiveness', by saying '**be perfect as your heavenly Father is**', he did not mean 'perfect' in a '**maximal sense**', which would be unattainable by human beings (p. 108). He meant: '**be all-inclusive in your *agape* as God is in his**' (p. 108). It is 'will' that is the key in both the '**man-to-God and man-to-man dimensions**' (p. 109). Look at Jesus. There have been few more 'unlovable' people than those who stood around his cross, but he said, 'Forgive them' (p. 109). As Paul expresses it, '**While we were yet sinners Christ**

died for us' (p. 109). The Christian love ethic is **'altruistic'**; it declares 'I will give, requiring nothing in return' (p. 110).

SELF-LOVE FOR THE NEIGHBOUR'S SAKE (pp. 110–14)

The primary nature of *agape* is 'other-regarding', but on occasions it may legitimately be 'self-regarding' (p. 110). However, consideration of the self is always for the 'neighbor's sake', not 'the self's' (p. 110). For we must ask, 'is self-love always selfish' (p. 110)? Do the claims of self always have to be denied? No. The 'logic of love' is that 'self-concern' should take priority over 'neighbor-good', whenever *'more* neighbor-good will be served through serving the self' (p. 113). We should serve the self in preference to a neighbour if, by doing so, *'many* neighbors are served' (p. 113). This parallels love's problem when one neighbour's good conflicts with another's. It is not that we prefer one neighbour to another. What we *'do* prefer' is the neighbour 'whose need is greater', and we 'prefer to serve *more* neighbors rather than fewer' (p. 113). Thus, the 'ship's captain or the plane's pilot' must preserve their own lives, even at the cost of some others, if 'disaster threatens all' (p. 113).

For Christians, self-love may be right or wrong: it depends on the good being sought and the situation. Loving ourselves 'for our own sakes' is always wrong, but loving ourselves for God's sake and the neighbour's is right (p. 114).

CALCULATION IS NOT CRUEL (pp. 114–19)

Moral choices need intelligence and accurate information, as much as they do concern and a 'good disposition' (p. 114). Only those who 'sentimentalize and subjectivize love' regard calculation as 'cold or cruel' and incompatible with 'love's warmth' (p. 116). **Tolstoy** wanted love to be 'futureless', and to take no account of 'consequences', seeing only the neighbour 'who is *there*'; but this is the 'soul of sentimentality' (p. 116). He would have instructed a doctor, hurrying to the scene of a major accident, involving tens or hundreds of people, to stop because a single motorist had crashed into a wall. Again, we must recognize that it is not the function of agapeic love 'to please' (p. 117). It is 'sentimental' and 'simplistic' to contend that love 'cannot or ought not calculate' (p. 118). Yes, love may mature, and become 'actualized', if a degree of fire is allowed to 'warm its work', but what it seeks most is not 'heat', but 'light': the 'heat it can leave to romance' (p. 119).

VII Love Justifies Its Means (pp. 120–33)

We almost despair when we see how Christian ethics, down the ages, has gone on insisting that the end does not justify the means. But this is absurd, and the same as saying that 'a thing is not worth what it costs' (p. 120).

WHAT JUSTIFIES A MEANS? (pp. 120–3)

Unless we have some purpose in mind to 'justify' it, our every action is 'literally meaningless' (p. 120). Means and ends are '*relative*' to each other, and with any action the '**coexistence of its means and ends**' puts it in the '**realm of ethics**' (p. 121).

While our 'loyalty' to our chosen end is stronger than that to the 'means we use', the latter must be 'appropriate' (p. 121). We can characterize our means as 'ingredients' of an action, not simply 'neutral tools', and we have an obligation to select them carefully (pp. 121–2). They are not 'ethically indifferent', and to be justified must, as H. R. Niebuhr observes, be *'fitting'* to the end (p. 122). However, we must remember that nothing is intrinsically 'good or evil' (p. 123). Thus, means that may be good in one situation, may be evil in another; what is 'sometimes wrong may sometimes be right when it serves a good enough end – *depending on the situation'* (p. 123).

LAW ENTANGLES ITSELF (pp. 123–7)

Situation ethics, the 'new morality', maintains that 'anything and everything is right or wrong, according to the situation' (p. 124). During World War Two, the French *maquis* resorted to murder, theft and lies in order to pursue their struggle against the Germans effectively. Was this permissible? In their view it was: in such circumstances, and for such an end, 'everything is permitted – and everything is forbidden' (p. 124). The problem for the proponents of the 'intrinsic theory of value' is that they are trapped into the 'untenable position' of having to rule out certain actions as absolutely wrong, irrespective of circumstances (p. 125). Lying or suicide, for example, are always unacceptable, even if they could produce 'a great deal of good' (p. 125). Such '**intrinsicalism**' can also involve condemning the lesser rather than the greater evil, as when someone is denounced for a loving deed, such as stealing a man's gun to stop him shooting another 'in anger' (p. 125).

An act is only justified if it has 'a loving purpose' (p. 125). **Theodore Roosevelt** was bogged down in 'intrinsicalist legalism' when he pronounced that 'No man is justified in doing evil on the ground of expediency' (pp. 125–6). On the contrary, 'love could justify anything', and nothing is justified, except by 'love's expedients' (p. 126). So why should a 'single woman', unable or unwilling to marry, not become a single parent, 'by **natural**

means or artificial insemination', if she chooses (p. 126)? Is it the case that 'an evil means' always nullifies 'a good end (p. 126)? On the basis of 'due proportion', the resounding answer must be '*No*': it 'always depends upon the situation' (p. 126).

THE FOUR FACTORS (pp. 127–31)

In every moral decision, there are four all-important factors, which must be 'balanced on love's scales': the end; the means; the motive; and the 'foreseeable *consequences*' (pp. 127–8). Traditional moralists often take the view that to be wrong an action has only to be at fault on 'one of these four scores', but to be right must be so 'on *all four*' (p. 128). Here we have, once more, to contend with '**universals and the categorical imperative**' (p. 128). However, as situationists we acknowledge 'no imperatives at all except *hypothetical* ones': an action becomes imperative '*only if* the situation demands it for love's sake' (pp. 128–9). The reality is that ends and means are mutually related in a '**contributory hierarchy**', such that each, in its turn, becomes a means to a higher end (p. 129). The only end, which is an 'end in itself', and not 'relative and contingent', is love (p. 129). Apart from love, the highest good, the '*summum bonum*', nothing is intrinsically good (p. 129).

There are moralists who always play the card of the '"**wedge" principle**' when there is any attempt to 'weigh relative values' (p. 130). They claim that allowing exceptions to a moral rule would create a dangerous precedent, and lead to general disobedience of it. They say this about, for example, **euthanasia**: if it were legalized, this 'would injure humanity' (p. 130). But we must see this kind of 'generalization argument' for what it is: a manoeuvre by opponents to discredit the situationist approach, thus undermining 'personal responsibility' and leaving 'law in control' (p. 131). This 'delaying action of static morality' is 'fundamentally antisituational' (p. 131).

HALLOWING THE MEANS (pp. 131–3)

It is a 'delusion' to believe that we can avoid the 'doubts and conflicts' of moral decision-making by 'turning to law', the inflexibility of which may result in a wrong action (p. 132). For example, a priest may learn from a confession that an innocent man is to die for another's crime. The priest can say nothing. But why should his 'rule of secrecy' be more 'sacrosanct' than the life of an innocent man on 'death row' (p. 132)?

Amid the 'relativities' of this world, the situationist holds that it is, on occasions, right to do 'what would be evil in some contexts', if, in this particular situation, it is what love demands (p. 132). Love must calculate the 'gains and losses', and decide (p. 132).

So it may be the case that, in this or that situation, the 'emotional and spiritual welfare' of the parents and children in a *particular* family' will be best met by divorce, 'wrong and cheap-jack' though divorce often is (p. 133).

VIII Love Decides There and Then (pp. 134–45)

Sometimes we behave as if, having made up our minds, we do not want to be confused by the facts.

WANTED: A SYSTEM (pp. 134–5)

A lot of people find moral laws reassuring: they are afraid of having too much freedom of grace. The situationist, in contrast, liberates himself from the 'dead hand of unyielding law', which falsely promises to remove the anxieties of moral decision-making (p. 135). As a 'free man', the situationist accepts all the 'ambiguities' of his freedom (p. 135).

THE GREY AREA (pp. 135–7)

When we grapple with 'real problems of conscience', we occupy a grey area, where there are no certainties (p. 135). But we have to examine all the facts thoroughly, and apply the love ethic to it. A woman in Arizona, having taken **thalidomide**, feared that her baby would be born with severe disabilities. With her doctor's support, she applied to the court for permission to terminate the pregnancy, but it refused, as state law prohibited '**nonmedically indicated abortions** without exception' (p. 136). So her husband took her to Sweden, where, as '**love has more control of law**', an abortion was performed. Hers was a 'brave and responsible' decision (p. 136).

Of course, this 'contextual, situational, clinical case method' offends some, as it is too 'full of variables' for their taste; they prefer the certainties of moral laws (pp. 136–7). But it is the situationist approach which matches up to the complexities of modern life and society. 'Prefab code morality' cracks under the pressure, and is revealed as a 'neurotic security device to simplify moral decisions': a task which it is incapable of performing (p. 137).

THE END OF IDEOLOGY (pp. 137–40)

Nothing creates more 'conflict of conscience' than continually paying lip-service to 'moral "laws"', which are forever being broken 'in practice' because their pettiness or rigidity prevents them fitting the 'facts of life' (pp. 137–8). Of course, there are many who prefer to try to 'fit reality to rules' rather than the other way round, and who favour order over freedom (p. 138). They would like to 'immobilize **Martin Luther King**' and his supporters, whereas situation ethics attaches the greater value to their freedom to protest (p. 138).

Christians today must not be so naive as to accept any view of Jesus apart from 'the situational one' (p. 139). There is nothing in his teachings about the 'ethics of sex, except adultery and an absolute condemnation of divorce' (p. 139). He says nothing about, for example, **homosexuality**, **sterilization**, **artificial insemination**, abortion or sex play. Whether any type of sex, 'hetero, homo, or auto', is right or wrong depends on 'whether love is fully served' (p. 139). With effective methods of contraception, we can have sex for '**re-creation as well as for procreation**'; and, if people do not think that sex outside marriage is wrong, 'it isn't, unless they hurt themselves, their partners, or others' (p. 140). Some maintain that situation ethics does not appreciate that most people have no wish to contend with the 'paradoxical ambiguities' of 'ethical relativism', and yearn for a few simple moral rules (p. 140). However, they are going to have to face up to the challenge.

FANATIC VIRTUE (pp. 141–3)

If it is the case that, as Jesus' Summary makes clear, actions are only right because they are loving, they are only right '*when* or while or as long as they are loving' (p. 141). An act's rightness does not lie in the act itself, but 'holistically' in the 'whole complex of all the factors in the situation, the total context'

(p. 141). Ecology studies the relationship between 'an organism and its environment', and we could say that situation ethics is an 'ecological ethics', as it takes account of a moral decision's 'context (environment)' (p. 142). This involves careful examination of the 'full play of ends, means motives, and result' (p. 142).

Let us take an example. Someone might ask the Christian situationist if a man should ever 'lie to his wife, or desert his family, or spy on a business rival's design or market plans, or fail to report some income item in his tax return' (p. 143). His response can only be a question of his own: 'Have you a *real* question, that is to say, a concrete situation?' (p. 143).

WHEN RIGHTS ARE RIGHT *(pp. 143–5)*

The facts show us what is the right or most loving thing to do; but once the relative course of action has been chosen, the 'obligation to pursue it is absolute' (p. 143). What the situationist has to find is 'absolute love's relative course' (p. 144).

Legal rights and prohibitions count for less than this. Following the law may sometimes be the most loving action, but there are other occasions 'when law denies love and destroys it' (p. 145). The essential point is that *'love's decisions are made situationally, not prescriptively'* (p. 145).

IX Postscriptum: Why? (pp. 146–59)

Is there any universal moral law? The situationist does not think so.

IX Postscriptum: Why?

A NEOCASUISTRY (pp. 146–50)

Situationism is the ethical approach in Christian ethics which fits 'our era's pragmatism and relativism' (p. 147). Further, it is 'neocasuistry' (p. 147). **G. E. Moore**, in *Principia Ethica*, writes that this is the 'goal of ethical investigation'; but if one is a thoroughgoing situationist, one will wish also to 'begin with cases', empirically (p. 147). Our neocasuistry is, like traditional casuistry, 'case-focused and concrete', and aims to 'bring Christian imperatives into practical operation' (p. 148).

Karl Barth has spoken of 'practical' or 'active casuistry', which involves 'understanding God's concrete specific command here and now'; and 'theological moralists' like Bonhoeffer, Barth and Brunner are 'clearheaded and plainspoken' about situation ethics' 'central thesis', which is the 'absoluteness of the word of love and the relativity of the deed', and recognition that an ethical decision's 'total context' is always 'circumstances under the law of love' (pp. 149–50).

NO MORE TABLETS OF STONE (pp. 150–2)

The formula of situation ethics is: '*the indicative plus the imperative equals the normative*' (p. 151). Love, in the 'imperative mood of neighbor-concern', examines the facts of the situation 'in the indicative mood', and identifies what it ought to do in the 'normative mood': 'what is, in the light of what love demands, shows what ought to be' (p. 151). Paul wrote to the Church at Philippi, 'And this I pray, that your love may abound yet more and more in knowledge and in all judgment' (p. 152). This covers the 'four pillars of the method of Christian ethics': '(1) a prayerful reliance upon God's grace; (2) the law of love as the norm; (3) knowledge of the facts, of the empirical situation in all its variety and relativity and particularity; and (4) judgment – i.e., decision – which is a matter of responsibility in humility' (p. 152).

ALLERGIC TO LAW *(pp. 152–4)*

Bishop John Robinson has observed that my exposition of situation ethics is bound to offend supporters of '**supernaturalistic legalism**' (p. 153). The important point of the new morality is that it looks forward: its focus is on 'facing forward toward moral choices yet to be made' (p. 153).

THE CHRISTIAN REASON WHY *(pp. 154–7)*

We have listed the four factors that all moral decisions involve: ends, means, motives and foreseeable results. Apart from the motive, there seems to be nothing 'unique' in the 'Christian's choices'; and even in this respect the motivating force behind non-Christian and even atheist decisions may be 'lovingness', which is not the monopoly of Christians (p. 155). As **C. S. Lewis** has commented, '. . . "Love Himself" . . . can work in those who know nothing of Him' (p. 155). Has not Bertrand Russell acknowledged that the world would be a better place for more 'Christian love or compassion' (p. 155)? What is special about the Christian's love is that it is 'a *responsive* love' of gratitude and 'thanksgiving to God', in particular for what he has done for human beings, through 'the **life, death and resurrection of Jesus Christ**' (p. 155). Without the 'doctrine of the **incarnation**', there is nothing 'special' about Christian ethics (p. 157). The incarnation enables us to understand what love is. It is not that we try to understand Jesus in terms of our own preconceived idea of what love is; rather, 'we understand love in terms of Jesus Christ' (p. 157).

THE QUESTION-ASKING WAY (pp. 157–9)

Christian ethics or moral theology is not a system by which we live 'according to a code' (p. 158). It requires a 'continuous effort' of relating love to 'a world of relativities through a casuistry obedient to love' (p. 158). We must be forever working out the 'strategy and tactics of love for Christ's sake' (p. 158). We must remember that God does not 'need our service' (p. 158). There is only one way that we can serve God, and that is by 'serving our neighbours'; and this is how we 'return his love' (p. 158).

X An Appendix: Two Other Corruptions and Four Cases (pp. 160–8)

Legalism is not the only corruption of Christian ethics, or cause of its having a bad name. The other two are '**pietism** and **moralism**' (p. 160).

PIETISM (pp. 160–1)

This is a distortion of piety. It divorces religion from ordinary life, and turns it into '**religiosity**': an '**internal "spiritual" or mystical affair**', which is held to have no concern with politics or business, including 'racial, or political justice' (p. 160). An inspiring example of the opposite of pietism is found in the career of the 'rector of a congregation of West Indians' in

Miami, who refused to hand over a membership list of the **'National Association for the Advancement of Colored People (NAACP)'** to the state legislature, because he knew that they planned to sack any in 'public service jobs' (p. 161). He suffered imprisonment, but his stand was ultimately vindicated in court.

MORALISM *(pp. 161–3)*

Legalism 'absolutizes law', pietism 'individualizes piety', while 'moralism trivializes morality' (p. 161). It makes much of such unimportant misdemeanours as dancing, playing cards and having fun on Sundays, but ignores the major moral questions. Jesus condemned this kind of pettiness in the Pharisees. We must also keep in the forefront of our minds the fact that it is not general ethical principles that are morally significant, but what we might call '*hyphenated* principles': for example, 'Love and a school integration'; 'love and an abortion following incest by force and violence'; or 'love and a hospital strike or a strike by doctors against **medical social security legislation**' (p. 163). Here are 'four actual cases' to consider (p. 163).

CHRISTIAN CLOAK AND DAGGER *(pp. 163–4)*

On a plane to New York, the young woman sitting next to me initiated a conversation, and said that she wanted to discuss a moral question with me. It turned out that she had been educated at 'church-related schools' and a good college, and had a successful career (p. 163). Her problem was that out of the blue one of 'our intelligence agencies' wanted her to take a job in Europe, in order to lure 'an enemy spy into blackmail' through sex (p. 163). She was not being pressurized, and knew Christian teaching about sex, but what should she do about this issue of '**patriotic prostitution** and personal integrity' (p. 164)? How should she balance the latter against her 'loyalty' as a US citizen (p. 164)?

SACRIFICIAL ADULTERY (pp. 164–5)

In the closing weeks of World War Two, a German woman whose husband was a prisoner of war in Britain was searching for food for her children. She was captured by the Russians, and sent to prison in the Ukraine. The woman wanted to get back to her family, including her now liberated husband, but there were only two grounds for her release: if she was seriously ill or if she became pregnant, in which case she would be regarded as a 'liability' (p. 165). She thought about it, and than asked a friendly 'camp guard' to make her pregnant (p. 165). Her condition was 'verified', and she was able to return to her family, who welcomed both her and subsequently the child she gave birth to: he had 'done more for them than anybody' (p. 165). Did she do the right thing, and was her family's reaction appropriate?

'HIMSELF MIGHT HIS QUIETUS MAKE' (pp. 165–6)

I was asked to visit Jim, an engineer, married with five children, who had been hospitalized due to the collapse of his 'digestive system' (p. 165). After further tests he told me that he had been given three years, at best; he could not work, and would need tablets costing $40 a day, which he could not afford, to keep him going at all. However, he had company life insurance of $100,000. If he did not take the tablets, and died within a short period of time, it would pay out double; but if he borrowed the money for medication, and lived on beyond the following autumn, the policy would not be renewed, and he would leave his family in 'the poor house' (p. 166). What, he wondered, was 'the right thing' for him to do (p. 166)?

SPECIAL BOMBING MISSION NO. 13 *(pp. 167–8)*

In the early morning of 6 August 1945, the United States bomber *Enola Gay* dropped a nuclear bomb on the Japanese city of Hiroshima. When it exploded, '**Captain Lewis** uttered six words, "My God, what have we done?"' (p. 167). Three days later another bomb fell on Nagasaki: tens of thousands were killed, 'wounded and burned'; and 'many times more' died subsequently (p. 167).

Though he was Vice President, Harry S. Truman knew nothing about the bomb until he succeeded **Franklin D. Roosevelt** as President. Most of his advisers thought he should use it, as did **Winston Churchill**. Others, including some of the 'nuclear physicists', and **Admiral Leahy**, were opposed (p. 167). They thought the Japanese should be given the chance to surrender, although 'intelligence experts' said nothing would induce them to do so (p. 167). In June 1945 the '**Interim Committee**' Truman had appointed to advise him on the matter reported, recommending the bomb's immediate use against both civilian and military targets, and without 'prior warning' (p. 168). At the 'final discussion' opinion was still divided (p. 168). Truman asked questions, but was as yet 'undeclared': but this was the 'moment of decision' (p. 168).

Overview

The following section is a chapter-by-chapter bullet-point summary of the main points in Fletcher's *Situation Ethics*. Designed for quick reference to the Detailed Summary above, readers may find it helpful for revision.

Foreword (pp. 11–16)

- To be true to its nature, Christian situation ethics cannot be a system: it is a method.
- Christian situationism tailors ethical decisions to fit objective circumstances, and stresses the normative ideal of love.

I Three Approaches (pp. 17–39)

- There are three ways of making moral decisions: legalistic, antinomian and situational.

APPROACHES TO DECISION-MAKING (pp. 18–31)
1 *Legalism (pp. 18–22)*

- Ethical legalism involves a set of fixed rules and regulations which can be looked up in a book, such as the Bible, and which rigidly prescribe certain actions, irrespective of the situation.
- In Christianity, ethical legalism has taken two forms.
- Roman Catholic moralists have applied human reason to the facts of nature, and based what they claim to be natural moral laws on nature (natural law).

- Protestants have been just as legalistic, but have based their moral law on biblical revelation.

2 Antinomianism (pp. 22–5)

- Ethical antinomianism rejects all principles or maxims whatsoever.
- Some moralists, including some Christians, claim to have a special radarlike faculty of moral intuition, which tells them the right thing to do.
- Sartre contends that, as life has no definite pattern, there is no justification for having moral rules: every situation is different.
- Antinomianism leads to moral decisions which are spontaneous but random.

3 Situationism (pp. 26–31)

- Ethical situationism means approaching every ethical decision with a respectful awareness of the community's ethical maxims, but not being bound by them.
- These ethical maxims may need to be modified or set aside altogether, if that serves love best.
- For the Christian ethical situationist, the only absolute moral norm is *agape*: loving God through the neighbour.
- Situationism recognizes that circumstances alter cases, and that in moral decisions situational variables have to be considered just as much as general principles.
- Christian situation ethics is case-focused and concrete, seeking to relate love to the actual situation.

PRINCIPLES, YES, BUT NOT RULES (pp. 31–7)

- The ethical situationist questions whether any two situations are ever sufficiently alike to justify an ethical rule or anything more than a cautious generalization.
- Therefore, the Christian situationist clashes with the legalism of traditional Christian ethics.
- The Christian situationist's sole moral principle is love, without any prefabricated recipes for what it means in practice.

ABORTION: A SITUATION (pp. 37–9)

- In Fletcher's example of a mentally ill girl, raped and made pregnant by a fellow patient in a mental institution, a moral legalist would resist abortion on the grounds that killing is absolutely wrong.
- The situationist, applying the law of love, would support abortion, even if there was no risk to her life, for the sake of her physical and mental health, and because no unwanted and unintended baby should be born.
- The situationist would argue that it would not be killing because there is no person or human life in an embryo.

II Some Presuppositions (pp. 40–56)

FOUR WORKING PRINCIPLES (pp. 40–52)
1 *Pragmatism (pp. 40–3)*

- Pragmatism is an important tool in making the right ethical decisions, because it is concerned with what works in practice.

- Pragmatism itself does not provide ethical norms or standards.
- We must choose our highest good for ourselves, and for Christians the absolute norm is love.

2 *Relativism (pp. 43–6)*

- The situationist's actions are right to the extent that they measure up to the ultimate criterion of agapeic love.
- The situationist must act lovingly, but has no absolute rules as to how to act.
- The right action in a particular situation depends on a responsible judgement of that situation.
- Such ethical relativism has been part of Christian ethics since the time of Jesus.

3 *Positivism (pp. 46–50)*

- In ethics, our highest good is, like the decision to believe in God, a choice, not the conclusion of a chain of reasoning.
- A utilitarian cannot prove that pleasure/happiness is the highest good, any more than a Christian can prove his faith that love is.
- For the situationist, moral choices may be vindicated in practice, but cannot be proved in theory.
- In Christian ethics, our affirmation that God is love establishes love as the fundamental value.

4 *Personalism (pp. 50–2)*

- In situation ethics, people, not things, are the centre of concern.

- Nothing is inherently good except when it is useful to love as it works for the sake of persons.
- We must keep in mind that Christian ethics is person-centred, because God is personal and created human beings in his own image.
- Following Kant, we must treat persons always as ends, never merely as means.
- Situation ethics is not concerned with what is good, but with how to do good and for whom: with how to do the most loving thing possible in the situation.

CONSCIENCE (pp. 52–6)

- Talk of conscience is just a way of referring to our efforts to make decisions creatively, constructively and fittingly.
- Conscience is concerned with future moral judgements, not passing judgement on actions already performed.
- Situation ethics means studying each ethical situation in all its contextual particularity.
- It keeps ethical principles sternly in their place, affirming only one general principle: to love God through the neighbour.

III Love Only Is Always Good (pp. 57–68)

NOMINAL GOOD (pp. 57–60)

- For God, what is valuable is whatever suits his love's needs and purposes.
- In Christian situation ethics, nothing has value in and of itself, but derives its value from the fact that it happens to help or harm persons.

- An action which is right in one situation may be wrong in another.

LOVE IS A PREDICATE *(pp. 60–4)*

- Love is not a substance, but a principle which expresses the sort of actions Christians should call good.
- We must so act as to produce more good or loving-kindness than would be produced by any alternative action.
- Being loving is a way of relating to persons and of using things.
- Being loving is the sole regulative principle of Christian ethics.
- God is love, and we must try to imitate him, and love our neighbours.
- The opposite of love is not hate but indifference.
- We must keep in mind the New Testament instruction to love people, not principles.

ONLY EXTRINSIC *(pp. 64–8)*

- Situation ethics opposes the view that there are objectively valid ethical laws and maxims.
- For example, if a lie is told unlovingly, it is wrong, but if it is told lovingly it is right.
- Right and wrong, good and bad are what happen to the things we say and do, depending on how much love is served in the situation.
- For traditional moralists, suicide and lying are always wrong, irrespective of circumstances, despite the fact that in a particular situation such actions may show loving concern.

- No law or principle of value is good in itself, not even life or truth.
- Only one thing is intrinsically good, namely, love.

IV Love Is the Only Norm (pp. 69–86)

- Christian situation ethics transforms morality from a statutory system of rules to the law of love.
- This is why Jesus disregarded the rules about not working on the Sabbath, and helped those in need.

LOVE REPLACES LAW (pp. 69–71)

- The situationist's response to the claim that love requires us to abide by strict moral rules is that he will only do so if it maximizes love.
- Often, love and moral rules conflict, and love only employs moral rules when it seems worthwhile to do so.

TABLETS OF STONE (pp. 71–5)

- This applies even to the Ten Commandments.
- Situation ethics maintains that on occasions we can break any or all of the Ten Commandments, including those which prohibit killing, adultery, stealing, false witness, and covetousness.
- We must exchange the legalist's love of law for the law of love.

NEITHER NATURE NOR SCRIPTURE *(pp. 75–7)*

- Situationism rejects every form of ethical legalism.
- To the supporters of Roman Catholic natural law legalism, situationists say that there are no universal ethical principles which all human beings have always followed.
- To the supporters of Protestant Scriptural legalism, situationists say that frustration is the only result of turning the Bible into a book of rules.

LOVE HAS NO EQUALS *(pp. 77–81)*

- Christian ethics is a situation ethic.
- Christian situation ethics is the new morality, which frees Christian conduct from rigid creeds and codes, and takes love as its source principle.
- The whole Christian ethic can be expressed as the single maxim: 'Love with care and then do what you will.'
- Christian *agape* is giving love which is non-reciprocal, neighbour-regarding, and includes even enemies.
- Situation ethicists, with love as their fundamental ethical principle, are both free and responsible.
- They are not bound by traditional Christian rules about sexual relationships, but must do the most loving thing.

OBJECTIONS *(pp. 81–6)*

- Critics claim that situation ethics requires more critical intelligence, factual information and thirst for righteousness than most people possess.
- They say it ignores the reality of human sin and the limitations of human reason.

- There is no denying that the situationist, particularly the Christian one, needs to be ethically mature and responsible.
- But it is cheap legalism to hide behind the letter of the law, for moral absolutes falsify the complex realities of ethical issues.
- Our opinions are only as good as our facts, so it is essential that we know all the facts of a situation before we act.
- As to the charge that situationism can mean rationalizing selfish motives, so too can the application of rigid moral rules.
- Selfish motives can hide as easily behind rules as behind free situational choices.

V *Love and Justice Are the Same (pp. 87–102)*

- Many ethical problems come down to the tension between love and justice.

LOVE IS CAREFUL (pp. 87–9)

- However, there need be no conflict between love and justice.
- With careful calculation, love can not only take justice into account, but become justice.
- Indeed, as what is due to our neighbours is love alone, love is justice and justice is love.
- Further, as justice means giving each person his due, we must distribute love as widely as possible.
- We have to be calculating, careful, prudent, distributive, and take everything into account, in order to maximize love and extend it to all.

WRONGFUL SEPARATION (pp. 89–92)

- Justice matters, because we are concerned with being loving to more than one person in what are sometimes extremely complex situations.
- For example, distributive or many-to-one justice may involve a community sharing out assets among its citizens, as in retirement benefits, and we have to decide how much love demands that each should receive.
- Equally difficult is contributive or one-to-many justice, as when we pay our taxes, and have to decide how much each individual should pay.
- We must always be mindful of the fact that Christian ethics involves adding an 's' to 'neighbour': *agape* does not mean loving only our immediate neighbour on a one-to-one basis.

A PROPOSED REUNION (pp. 92–5)

- For the Christian situationist, there is no problem of justice versus love.
- For the Christian situationist, to be just is to be loving.
- The Christian situationist rejects the view that love and justice are alternatives, with love transcendent and impossible, and justice relative and possible.
- Rather, love is maximum justice and justice is optimum love.
- Justice is simply love working out its problems.
- As for human rights, the situationist's position is that what the neighbour is entitled to is anything that is loving and nothing that is unloving.

- All rights, including such fundamental ones as religious freedom, free speech, public assembly, private property, sexual liberty, life itself, the vote, are contingent and relative, and justified only by love.

LOVE USING ITS HEAD (pp. 95–9)

- Justice is love coping with situations which require the distribution of love.
- To do so, the love ethic must follow the example of the utilitarians' hedonic calculus.
- It must develop an agapeic calculus, designed to calculate the greatest quantity of lovingness for the largest number of neighbours possible.
- Although situation ethics' concern with maximizing good has more in common with consequentialist ethics, it can also be understood in terms of deontological or duty ethics.
- The situationists' duty is to maximize love in every situation.
- This involves an unsentimental approach to tough ethical decisions.
- For example, a doctor who gives his last available unit of blood plasma to a mother of three rather than an old alcoholic, is using his judgement in order to apply love appropriately to a specific situation.
- Love means examining each situation carefully, and calculating how much love our choices will produce.
- This is what President Truman did in his decision to drop atomic bombs on Hiroshima and Nagasaki.

ADDENDUM (pp. 99–102)

- Situationists accept the need for law and order, as long as they promote the interests of love.
- However, justice must be understood agapeically, and laws may be right or wrong.
- The Christian situationist's duty is to obey or disobey the law, depending on what best serves the basic principle of love.

VI Love Is Not Liking (pp. 103–19)

- Christian love is about attitudes, not feelings.

NEVER SENTIMENTALIZE LOVE (pp. 103–7)

- A young, unmarried Christian couple may decide to have a sexual relationship, but they must have loving concern for each other.
- Christian love or *agape* is primarily an active determination of the will, not an emotion, like ordinary love; so, unlike a feeling, it can be commanded.
- Christian love is benevolence or goodwill, and its opposite is not hatred, but indifference.
- Christian love extends to our neighbours not, ultimately, for our or their sakes, but for God's.
- Christians cannot compel themselves to like everybody, but they can compel themselves to be kind, generous, merciful, patient, concerned to/about others.

THE NEIGHBOUR IS ANYBODY (pp. 107–10)

- As Christians, we must love not only the stranger-neighbour and the acquaintance-neighbour, but also the enemy-neighbour, as we love the friend-neighbour.
- Christians must be all-inclusive in their love, as God is in his.
- The Christian love ethic is altruistic: it gives, expecting and requiring nothing in return.

SELF-LOVE FOR THE NEIGHBOUR'S SAKE (pp. 110–14)

- Christian love is primarily other-regarding, but may legitimately be self-regarding, for the neighbour's sake.
- The logic of love is that self-concern should take priority over neighbour-concern, whenever more neighbour-good will be produced by serving the self.
- For example, a ship's captain or a plane's pilot must preserve their own lives, even at the cost of some other people, if disaster threatens all.
- For Christians, self-love may be right or wrong, depending on the situation.
- Loving ourselves for the sake of God and the neighbour is right.

CALCULATION IS NOT CRUEL (pp. 114–19)

- Doing the most loving thing requires careful calculation, and only those who sentimentalize love regard calculation as incompatible with love's warmth.
- For example, it would be sentimental and simplistic to ask a doctor, hurrying to the scene of a major accident, involving many people, to stop and help a single injured motorist.

VII *Love Justifies Its Means (pp. 120–33)*

- Christian ethics has been wrong to insist that the end does not justify the means.

WHAT JUSTIFIES A MEANS? *(pp. 120–3)*

- In ethical decisions, while loyalty to the chosen end is stronger than to the means, the latter must be appropriate and chosen carefully.
- However, as nothing is intrinsically good or evil, means that may be good in one situation may be evil in another: it all depends on the situation.

LAW ENTANGLES ITSELF *(pp. 123–7)*

- Situation ethics, the new morality, maintains that anything and everything is right or wrong, according to the situation.
- Even murder, theft and lies may be permissible in certain situations, as by the French resistance movement during World War Two.
- But the advocates of the intrinsic theory of value are forced to rule out certain actions as absolutely wrong, irrespective of circumstances and even if they produce good.
- And this intrinsicalism can mean condemning a lesser, rather than a greater, evil.
- Love could justify anything, and nothing is justified, except by love.
- Thus, depending on the situation, a single woman, unable or unwilling to marry, could be justified in choosing to become a single parent, by natural means or artificial insemination.

82

THE FOUR FACTORS *(pp. 127–31)*

- Every moral decision involves four all-important factors: the end, the means, the motive and the foreseeable consequences.
- However, an action does not have to be right on all these scores in order to be the right action in the situation.
- For the only thing that matters is love, which is the only end in itself, the only thing which is intrinsically good, and the only test which an action has to pass.
- Some moralists argue that allowing exceptions to a moral rule would create a dangerous precedent, and lead to general disobedience of it.
- They claim, for example, that euthanasia, if legalized, would injure humanity.
- But this kind of generalization is just designed by opponents to discredit the situationist approach.

HALLOWING THE MEANS *(pp. 131–3)*

- It is an error to think that the doubts and conflicts of moral decision-making can be avoided by applying moral rules, whose inflexibility may lead to wrong actions.
- For example, a priest may learn at confession that an innocent man is to die for another's crime.
- He can say nothing, so his rule of secrecy then takes precedence over the life of an innocent man on death row.
- The situationist believes that it is sometimes right to do what would be evil in some contexts, if it is what love demands in the particular situation.
- Thus, in their particular circumstances, the needs of a particular family may be best met by divorce, wrong and squalid though divorce often is.

VIII *Love Decides There and Then (pp. 134–45)*

- People making ethical decisions sometimes behave as if they do not want to be confused by the facts.

WANTED: A SYSTEM (pp. 134–5)

- Many people find moral rules reassuring, as they fear moral freedom.
- But the situationist rejoices in being free of the dead hand of inflexible moral rules, which promise falsely to remove the anxieties of moral decision-making.

THE GREY AREA (pp. 135–7)

- In moral decisions, there are no certainties.
- Moral decisions require thorough examination of all the facts, and application of the love ethic to them.
- A woman who had taken thalidomide feared that her baby would be born with severe disabilities, but the law in her state allowed abortions only when there was a risk to the pregnant woman's life.
- She went to Sweden, where love had more influence on the law, and had an abortion.
- Of course, there are those who prefer the certainties of moral laws.
- But it is situationism which matches up to the complexities of modern life and society.

THE END OF IDEOLOGY (pp. 137–40)

- Nothing causes more moral confusion than lip-service being paid to moral rules, which are always being broken, because they are too rigid to fit the facts of life.

- Those who try to fit reality to the moral rules show that they prefer order to freedom.
- Christians must appreciate that Jesus' approach was a situational one.
- He says nothing about the ethics of sex, except adultery and divorce, or about homosexuality, sterilization, artificial insemination or abortion.
- Whether any type of sex is right or wrong depends on whether love is served.
- Effective contraception makes possible sex for recreation as well as procreation.
- Extra-marital sex is only wrong if it hurts the people involved.
- People may want a few definite moral rules, but they have to face up to the challenges of life.

FANATIC VIRTUE (pp. 141–3)

- An act's rightness lies in the whole complex of all the factors in the situation.
- Situation ethics takes account of each moral decision's total individual context or environment.
- A Christian situationist cannot answer hypothetical questions about, for example, whether someone should desert his family, or spy on a business rival's design.
- His response will be to ask whether the enquirer has a specific, concrete situation in mind.

WHEN RIGHTS ARE RIGHT (pp. 143–5)

- Following moral rules may sometimes be the most loving thing to do, but there are situations where moral rules can destroy love.

- The essential point is that love's decisions are made situationally, not prescriptively.

IX Postscriptum: Why? (pp. 146–59)

- Situationists do not think that there is any universal moral law.

A NEOCASUISTRY (pp. 146–50)

- Situationism is the Christian ethical approach which suits the pragmatism and relativism of the age.
- It is a form of casuistry, because it is concerned with what to do in specific, concrete situations.

NO MORE TABLETS OF STONE (pp. 150–2)

- For the situationist, the situation as it is, examined in the light of love, shows what he ought to do.
- The method of Christian ethics has four pillars.
- The first is prayerful reliance on God's grace.
- The second is to have the law of love as the norm.
- The third is to know the facts of the situation in all its variety, relativity and particularity.
- The fourth is to exercise responsible and humble judgement.

ALLERGIC TO LAW (pp. 152–4)

- A key point about the new morality is that it looks forward to moral choices that have yet to be made.

Overview

THE CHRISTIAN REASON WHY *(pp. 154–7)*

- All moral decisions involve ends, means, motives and foreseeable results.
- Even as concerns motive, there may be nothing unique about Christian decisions.
- Lovingness is not a Christian monopoly, and may be the motivating force behind non-Christian and even atheist decisions.
- What is special about Christian love is that it is a love of gratitude to God, particularly for what he has done for human beings, through Jesus' life, death and resurrection.
- It is the incarnation which enables us to understand what love is.

THE QUESTION-ASKING WAY *(pp. 157–9)*

- Christian ethics requires a continuous effort to relate love to a world of relativities.
- The only way that human beings can serve God is by serving our neighbours, which is how we return his love.

X *An Appendix: Two Other Corruptions and Four Cases (pp. 160–8)*

- In addition to legalism, pietism and moralism are also corruptions of Christian ethics.

PIETISM *(pp. 160–1)*

- Pietism individualizes piety.

- It wrongly divorces religion from ordinary life, and turns it into a mystical affair, which is not concerned with politics or business.

MORALISM (pp. 161–3)

- Whereas legalism absolutizes law, moralism trivializes morality.
- It dwells on insignificant misdemeanours, such as dancing, playing cards and having fun on Sundays, but ignores the major moral questions.
- An important point to keep in mind is that it is not general ethical principles, but what could be called 'hyphenated' principles that really count.
- Examples are love and an abortion following incest by force and violence, or love and a strike by doctors against unfair medical social security legislation.

CHRISTIAN CLOAK AND DAGGER (pp. 163–4)

- Should a young woman agree to a request by the United States' security services that she serve her country by using sex, in order to enable it to blackmail a spy?

SACRIFICIAL ADULTERY (pp. 164–5)

- Was a German woman in a Russian prison camp right to get a guard to make her pregnant, so that she would be released and reunited with her family?
- Was her family right to be happy that she did?

Overview

'HIMSELF MIGHT HIS QUIETUS MAKE' (pp. 165–6)

- Would a terminally ill husband and father be right to deny himself medical treatment, and hasten his own death, in order to ensure that his family received death benefits under his life insurance policy, when the alternative would be to leave them penniless?

SPECIAL BOMBING MISSION NO. 13 (pp. 167–8)

- In the light of all the circumstances of the situation, was President Harry S. Truman right to authorize the dropping of atom bombs on Hiroshima and Nagasaki?

Glossary

A-bombs on Hiroshima and Nagasaki. The dropping of atomic bombs on the Japanese cities of Hiroshima and Nagasaki, on the orders of President Truman (see below), in August 1945. The argument was that it would bring the war with Japan to an end more quickly, and avoid the lives of Allied soldiers being lost in a full-scale invasion of Japan. However, the decision was opposed by some of Truman's advisers, and it has been contended that Japan would have been willing to surrender without the use of atomic weapons. Fletcher discusses Truman's decision in more detail in Chapter X.

Abortion. Here Fletcher discusses a situation where the inflexibility of a US state's laws prohibiting abortion, except on 'therapeutic' grounds (serious risk to the pregnant woman's life or health), rule out an abortion in circumstances where it is in the interests of all concerned. However, Fletcher also states that an abortion is permissible because an embryo, at an early stage of development, has no intrinsic value: but this is the very point that a Roman Catholic moral theologian, for example, would contest.

Acquaintance-neighbour. Somebody known only slightly.

Active determination of the will. Agapeic love is not primarily to do with how we feel about another person, or other people. It is an attitude of loving concern for their well-being as fellow human beings, who have been made by God in his own image. Therefore, unlike ordinary love, agapeic love can be controlled by the will: it is the attitude Christians ought to have towards other people.

Advisers without veto power (ethical principles as). Fletcher maintains that situationists should respect established ethical principles, and use them as guides when making moral decisions, but should not be bound by them. There will be occasions when the most loving thing to do conflicts with an established ethical principle, such as 'do not lie' or 'do not steal'.

Glossary

Agape. 1 John 4.11–12 declares: 'if God so loved us, we ought to love one another'. Christian love or *agape* for other people reflects God's love for us. Unlike ordinary human love, it is unconditional and does not depend on the desirableness of the other person, or on their being family members or friends. It is a giving love, which seeks the good of the other person(s), simply because they are human beings, created by God. For Fletcher, *agape* is the key element in every moral decision.

Agapeic calculus. Fletcher suggests that situation ethicists should copy utilitarians (see Hedonistic calculus below). In a situation requiring a moral choice, they should try to calculate how much 'neighbour welfare' possible actions will produce, and perform the action which will produce the most. However, as well as the problem of calculating all the consequences of any action, it seems particularly difficult to determine which action would be the most loving, or would produce the most love; and certainly, unlike Bentham, Fletcher does not suggest any mechanism for doing so. Therefore, the judgement is bound to be a subjective one.

Agapeic love. See *Agape* above.

Aggressive, questing prudence of *agape*. It is not enough to make non-maleficence our main ethical principle, and just refrain from causing harm to others. Situationists must be proactive: they must look for opportunities to behave lovingly towards others, and to promote their well-being. However, they must also be prudent, and assess each situation carefully, to ensure that they perform the action which is the most loving in that particular situation.

Altruistic. The Christian love ethic is unselfish: those who practise it put the needs and well-being of others above their own.

American pragmatism. The theory of truth, associated particularly with the American philosophers William James (see below) and Charles Peirce (see below), which, in various formulations, identifies the meaning of a doctrine with its practical results: how it affects conduct, or whether it 'works' for the person who believes it. Fletcher argues that an important feature of Christian situationism is that it passes the test set by pragmatism: it is successful in practice. However, pragmatism does not supply the objects of Christian situationism, or the criteria by which its success is judged. These are provided by the Christian ethic of love.

Anglo-American principle of minding your own business. It is easy to criticize this negative principle, but non-maleficence, the principle of refraining from causing harm to others, is essential to the existence of a civilized society. See also Aggressive, questing prudence of *agape* above.

Antecedent rather than consequent conscience. Fletcher regards conscience as moral awareness, the function of which is to focus on moral decisions that are going to be made and to ensure that they maximize love. He is critical of a view of conscience which sees its role as reviewing and identifying the shortcomings of decisions already made.

Antinomian (approach to morals). Fletcher regards this as the complete opposite of (moral) legalism (see below). The antinomian ignores any guidance that established ethical principles or rules may offer about moral decisions. Christians, who consider themselves to have been saved by faith in Christ, and to be possessed by the Holy Spirit, sometimes adopt this attitude.

Arbitrary and absurd as the leap of faith. There is (Fletcher maintains) a limit to what reason can accomplish in ethics. It can establish facts, and infer the relations between them, but it cannot ultimately 'prove' that one set of moral values or principles is better than another: any more than it can 'prove' that God exists and that people should believe in him. Fundamental or first moral principle(s) are, like the decision to believe in God, a matter of choice, a leap of faith. However, some moral philosophers, such as Plato, hold that there is a transcendental basis for moral values, which exists at a different level of reality, or that moral values are logically grounded in human needs, and that actions which harm other human beings are always wrong.

Aristotle (384–322 BC). Greek philosopher, student of Plato, and author of such books as *Metaphysics, De Interpretatione* and *The Nicomachean Ethics*. In the last-mentioned, Aristotle explains that people will lead happy and well-balanced lives (*eudaimonia*) if they fulfil their nature as rational beings, and practise the intellectual and moral virtues.

Artificial insemination. Becoming pregnant by means other than sexual intercourse, such as in vitro fertilization (IVF).

Augustine, Saint (354–430). Christian philosopher and theologian, and Bishop of Hippo in North Africa. His works include *Confessions* and *City of God*.

Axiomatic value. Agapeic love is the self-evident value in Christian ethics.

Backbone of all legalism. Fletcher's contention, throughout *Situation Ethics*, is that there are no intrinsically right or wrong actions. Even things that are usually (regarded as) wrong, such as lying or stealing, may sometimes be right, that is, the most loving thing to do, in a particular situation. The idea that some things are intrinsically wrong is at the root of (moral) legalism.

Barth, Karl (1886–1968). Influential Swiss Protestant theologian, who taught at the German universities of Gottingen, Münster and Bonn, but was forced to move to Basle when he refused to take an oath of loyalty to Hitler. Barth's theology emphasizes human beings' sinfulness and need for God's grace. His writings include the multi-volume *Church Dogmatics*, the first part of which was published in 1932, and a commentary, *The Epistle to the Romans* (1919).

Be all-inclusive in your agape **as God is in his**. God's love embraces all human beings, and Christians must not be selective about whom they love: their *agape* must apply to all human beings, including strangers and enemies, not just to family and friends.

Be perfect as your heavenly Father is (Matthew 5.48). Fletcher explains that this refers to the Christian's love being all-inclusive. See above.

Benevolence. Good will, wishing to do good. *Agape* love actively promotes the welfare of others.

Bentham, Jeremy (1748–1832). The founder of utilitarianism, Bentham sought, through his writings (in particular, *An Introduction to the Principles of Morals and Legislation*) and example, to establish the greatest happiness principle as the accepted end of human action and the criterion of morality. Like utilitarianism, (Christian) situation ethics is a consequentialist ethic, but the good it promotes is the maximization of love, not pleasure/happiness.

Biblical revelation.. Here, the moral rules which it is believed that God has chosen to disclose to human beings through the Bible, and which must be adhered to. Fletcher explains that this, not natural law (see below), is the basis of Protestant (moral) legalism.

Bioethics. The philosophical study of the ethical issues raised by new developments in medicine and biology.

Bonhoeffer, Dietrich (1906–45). German theologian and Lutheran pastor, who was executed by the Nazis for participating in the resistance to Hitler. In both his life and his writings, which include *Act and Being* (1931), *The Cost of Discipleship* (1937) and *Ethics* (published 1949), Bonhoeffer emphasizes the 'costliness' of the grace Christians receive from God. They must obey Jesus, and be prepared to undergo the kind of sacrifice and suffering he endured.

Glossary

British empiricism. This tradition originated in the work of John Locke (1632–1704), George Berkeley (1685–1753) and David Hume (1711–76). Empiricists maintain that human beings do not have any innate knowledge, so experience is their main or only source of knowledge of the world. Situation ethics also emphasizes the importance of experience: how to act cannot be determined beforehand, only in the light of the actual situation.

Brunner, Heinrich Emil (1889–1966). Swiss Protestant theologian and professor at the University of Zurich, two of whose best-known works are *The Mediator* (1927) and *Revelation and Reason* (1946).

Casuistry. Working out detailed ethical rules, which cover conduct in specific situations and circumstances rather than depending on general ethical principles to guide conduct.

Categorical (moral decisions). Unconditional or absolute. The situation ethicist's moral decisions cannot be unconditional or absolute: he must always follow the course of action which he thinks will maximize love, and this will depend on all the relevant circumstances of a particular situation.

Categorical imperative. Kant's term for the imperative of morality, which commands unconditionally. What it commands must be done for its own sake, and because it is right, not in order to accomplish some further purpose; and it may conflict with a person's inclinations. Kant gives five different formulations of the categorical imperative in his *Groundwork of the Metaphysics of Morals*, the first of which is: 'Act only in accordance with that maxim through which at the same time you can will that it become a universal law.'

Catholic moral theology/theologian. The study of moral philosophy and ethics from the point of view of the Roman Catholic Church, which is informed by Roman Catholic teaching and ethics. 'Moral theology' is the academic study of moral philosophy/ethics from a Christian standpoint, but the term is not in general use outside the Roman Catholic Church.

Chastity. Refraining from sexual relationships/intercourse, particularly before marriage. In certain religions, including Christianity, chastity (and lifelong celibacy, for those who wish to devote their lives to God's service) is traditionally encouraged and valued.

C-love. Christian love (see *Agape* above).

Christian sex relations (marital monopoly). This kind of questioning of established Christian values made situation ethics unpopular with traditional Christian ethicists and church members. Fletcher argues that Christian men and women do not need to get married in order to have sexual relations with each other: any form of relationship is acceptable, provided they behave in the most loving way towards each other. The traditionalist response is that marriage, and the commitment it involves, is an essential element in the Christian way of life, and that other forms of relationship are less likely to endure.

Churchill, Sir Winston Leonard Spencer (1874–1965). A minister and Cabinet member of Liberal, Coalition and Conservative governments under Asquith, Lloyd George, Baldwin and Chamberlain. Prime minister of the wartime Coalition government, 1940–45, and Conservative prime minister, 1951–55. He supported the use of atomic weapons against Japan, and said that he did not doubt the rightness of President Truman's decision.

Classical moralists. Fletcher is referring to traditional (Christian) moralists, who hold that certain actions are intrinsically wrong and can never be justified by circumstances.

Classical pacifism. The view that violence and war are always wrong. Fletcher argues that such pacifists are relieved of having to make difficult ethical decisions about the kind of circumstances that justify going to war.

Coexistence of its means and ends puts it in the realm of ethics. For the situation ethicist, the end is always the maximization of love. Ethical decisions involve choosing the best means to achieve that end. Generally, Fletcher suggests that any means that achieve that end are acceptable, but on occasions suggests that some means may be inappropriate.

Collection of scattered sayings.. It is generally accepted by New Testament scholars that the Sermon on the Mount (Matthew 5—7) was not delivered as a continuous sermon by Jesus, on one occasion, but is a collection of Jesus' ethical teachings, which he delivered on different occasions.

Conscience (moral consciousness) as a function not a faculty. Unlike Cardinal Newman, who regarded the conscience as 'a voice, or the echo of a voice, imperative and constraining' (*A Grammar of Assent*), Fletcher regards it as a function of the reason, and no more than a convenient way of referring to human awareness of the need to make the most loving decisions.

Consequentialist ethic. One which determines the rightness or wrongness of an action on the basis of its consequences. The best-known consequentialist ethical system is utilitarianism, which judges actions to be right or wrong, according to whether or not they maximize pleasure/happiness, which utilitarians regard as the ultimate good. Situation ethics is also a consequentialist system, which aims at promoting the ultimate good of lovingness. One major problem with any consequentialist system, which Fletcher seems to ignore, is the difficulty of calculating all the consequences, over time, of any action we perform.

Context/contextual particularity. The situationist must study every aspect of a situation carefully, to ensure that he has considered every morally relevant factor, before he decides what to do.

Contributory hierarchy. Situation ethics does not rule out in principle any means of achieving its ultimate end. For the situation ethicist, intermediate ends become means towards the only end that is an end in itself: love.

1 Corinthians 6.12–20. In this passage, Paul argues against the antinomian approach to ethics, as practised by members of the Christian Church in Corinth, on both deontological and consequentialist grounds: the activities are wrong in themselves and also have bad consequences. Fletcher refers approvingly to what Paul has to say, but critics of situation ethics have argued either that situationism is a form of antinomianism, or that it creates a slippery slope into it. What Fletcher has to say about sexual relations and marriage (see above) gives substance to these criticisms.

Cox, Harvey Gallagher Jnr (b. 1929). Baptist minister and Hollis Professor of Divinity at Harvard Divinity School, whose books include the best-selling *The Secular City* (1965).

Created men in his own image. According to Genesis 1.26a, 27, God made human beings in his own image, so they are different from the rest of creation. As rational beings they have a special relationship with him; and this special status has important ethical implications, as human life is precious to God and uniquely valuable. This is the basis of the Christian doctrine of the sanctity of human life.

Cummings, Edward Estlin (1894–1962). American poet, essayist and novelist. Fletcher's reference is to Cummings' Charles Eliot Norton lectures in 1952–53.

Deontological ethics. An ethical system which holds that rightness has little or nothing to do with an action's consequences, and everything to do with the action itself; and that we have a duty to perform certain actions, such as keeping promises, telling the truth, and not harming others, because of their intrinsic rightness. The best-known deontological system is that of Immanuel Kant, who argues that all rational beings, which includes human beings, have absolute worth, and have an obligation to treat each other always as ends in themselves, never merely as means.

Dispositions of the will. Human beings cannot be ordered to have a particular feeling, such as liking them, towards other people; feelings cannot be commanded. However, dispositions or attitudes can be commanded, because they are under the control of the human will. Human beings, and Christian situationists in particular, must develop attitudes of kindness, generosity, mercy, patience, and so on, towards others, and act accordingly.

Divine Command. God commands human beings to be loving towards other people, but what this means in practice, how we maximize love in a particular situation, will depend on all the morally relevant circumstances of that situation.

Dodd, Charles Harold (1884–1973). British New Testament scholar and Congregationalist minister, who was Rylands Professor of Biblical Criticism and Exegesis at Manchester and Norris Hulse Professor of Divinity at Cambridge. He was General Director of the translation of the *New English Bible*, and his books include *The Apostolic Preaching and its Development* (1936), *The First Epistle of John and the Fourth Gospel* (1937) and *The Founder of Christianity* (1970).

Dogmatism. Generally, treating something as true despite evidence to the contrary. Here, Fletcher is criticizing the view that there are absolute ethical principles, which should always be followed, irrespective of the actual situation.

Editor-compiler of Matthew's Sermon on the Mount. See Collection of scattered sayings above. It is believed that, in addition to Mark's Gospel (generally thought to be the oldest Gospel) and sources unique to themselves, the authors of Matthew's and Luke's Gospels used a common source, referred to as 'Q', which contained many of the teachings of Jesus that are found in Matthew's Sermon on the Mount. There are a hundred plus verses in Matthew 5—7, and around half closely resemble verses in the 'Sermon on the Plain' in Luke's Gospel (Luke 6.20–49). However, there are different views among New Testament scholars, about the relationship between and dating of the three Synoptic Gospels (Mark, Matthew and Luke), which contain a great deal of common material.

Enemy-neighbour. As Matthew 5.43–48 makes clear, Jesus expects Christians to love their enemies, and treat them as neighbours.

Enola Gay. The name given to the B29 Super Fortress bomber which dropped the atomic bomb on Hiroshima on 6 August 1945. The aeroplane is now on display at the National Air Space Museum's Steven F. Udvar-Hazy Center, outside Washington.

Episcopal Church. The Episcopal Church of the United States of America: the Anglican Church in the United Sates.

Ethical relativism. The view that there are no absolute ethical principles or standards, which apply to every situation: each situation is different, and even basic ethical principles, such as those condemning theft, or even killing, may need to be set aside, if the circumstances demand it.

Eugenics. The study of ways of improving, or view that attempts should be made to improve, the qualities of the human species. Eugenics can be divided into negative eugenics, which seeks to discourage breeding by those with genetic defects, or who are considered likely to transmit undesirable qualities, and positive eugenics, which seeks to encourage breeding by those thought likely to transmit desirable qualities. The eugenics movement had strong support in the United States and Britain during the late nineteenth and early twentieth centuries, but was accused of racism and class bias, and was discredited by Nazi eugenics experiments during World War Two.

Euthanasia. Fletcher was an advocate of voluntary euthanasia. This would allow doctors and others to help those in extreme pain and/or suffering from a terminal illness, who wished to end their suffering, to die a 'gentle and easy' death, for example by injecting them with a lethal drug. This is currently the situation in the Netherlands, but voluntary euthanasia is illegal elsewhere. It is condemned by the Christian Churches as contrary to Christian teaching about the sanctity of human life (see Created men in his own image above). Here, Fletcher challenges the view often argued by opponents of voluntary euthanasia that legalizing it would insert a 'wedge' into general respect for/legal protection of human life, and lead on to non-voluntary or involuntary euthanasia, where people's lives are ended without their consent or against their wishes.

Existentialism. Philosophical approach which holds that as the world lacks (or appears to) an ultimate purpose, and does not offer human beings a clear set of beliefs, values or purposes, individuals must choose these for themselves.

Extrinsicalism of situation ethics. The view that nothing (apart from the ethic of love) is intrinsically good or bad, or right or wrong.

Faith propositions are affirmed voluntaristically. See Theological positivism below.

Glossary

Faith working through love. In Galatians 5.6, Paul explains that the only thing that matters is faith in God, which shows itself in loving behaviour towards other people. Complying with religious rules and regulations is unimportant: 'neither circumcision nor uncircumcision is of any avail, but faith working through love.'

Free contextual choices. The situationist must disregard ethical rules, if necessary, and do the most loving thing. Fletcher rejects his critics' argument that situationism is more likely to be used as a cover for selfishly motivated actions than any other ethical approach, including rules-based, traditional morality.

Friend-neighbour. People have little difficulty treating their friends, about whose welfare they are concerned, as neighbours. The challenge for Christians is to regard and treat strangers and enemies in the same way.

Friendship love (*philia*). The love people feel for their friends/those important to them, with whom they have things in common, and who play a major part in their lives, as distinct from *agape* (see above) or *eros* (see Romantic love below).

Fruits of the Spirit. In Galatians 5.22, Paul lists Christian virtues, which flow from belief in God, and being filled with his Holy Spirit. They are: love, joy, peace, patience, kindness, goodness, faithfulness, gentleness and self-control.

Gnostics. *Gnosis* is the Greek word for 'knowledge', and adherents of this heresy, which was widespread in the fourth century, claimed to have special, intuitive knowledge of the meaning of Jesus' teaching, and so did not feel the need to heed the Church's interpretation of it, or to abide by its rules.

God is love. Christians believe that God is omnibenevolent or all-loving, and that Christians must reflect God's love for them in their own lives: 'Beloved, let us love one another; for love is of God, and he who loves is born of God and knows God. He who does not love does not know God for God is love' (1 John 4.7–8).

Grace and freedom. In Christian teaching, grace is the help God freely gives to human beings through Jesus Christ. Fletcher believes that Christians should use this grace to help them exercise their judgement, and make the most loving decision in each situation; they should not just depend on generally accepted ethical principles and rules.

Grace, the new life in Christ and salvation by faith. Christians believe that in spite of their sins, through their faith in Jesus, whose death has atoned for their sins and whose resurrection promises life beyond physical death, they can be reconciled to God and receive eternal life. However, as in the Church at Corinth (see 1 Corinthians 6 above), some Christians believe that because they have received salvation through faith, they can behave as they please and ignore their responsibilities to others.

Hare, Richard Mervyn (1919–2002). Moral philosopher and White's Professor of Moral Philosophy at Oxford (1966–83), whose books include *The Language of Morals* (1952), *Freedom and Reason* (1963) and *Moral Thinking* (1891).

Hatfield, Forrest (1905–88). Joseph Fletcher's wife and a campaigner for contraception and birth control. They met as students at West Virginia University.

Hedonistic/hedonic calculus (or felicific calculus). In his *Introduction to the Principles of Morals and Legislation* (Chapter 4), Jeremy Bentham explains how to calculate the quantity of pleasure or pain that a particular action will produce, and thus to decide whether it is the right one. The main factors to be taken into account are intensity, duration, certainty/uncertainty and propinquity/remoteness. In fact, this apparently scientific approach does not remove the difficulty of working out the consequences of actions over time.

History of Western morals. The history of ethics and moral philosophy in the western tradition, from Plato and Aristotle onwards.

Hitler, Adolf (plot to kill). This was the plot (July 1944), conceived by high-ranking officers in the Wermacht (German Army) but with which others, such as Dietrich Bonhoeffer (see above), were associated, to assassinate Hitler, seize control of the German government and negotiate terms with the western Allies (the United States and Britain). A bomb was placed in Hitler's military headquarters at Rastenburg, East Prussia by Colonel Claus von Stauffenburg, but did not kill Hitler. Those involved in the plot were arrested and executed.

Homosexuality. Attitudes to homosexuality and gay rights were very different in the 1950s and early 1960s. *Situation Ethics* was published in 1966, before the passing of the Sexual Offences Act 1967 in Britain, which legalized homosexual acts in private, between two consenting adults who had reached the age of twenty-one.

Hume, David (1711–76). Perhaps the greatest British philosopher, whose empirical approach to philosophy and reputation for scepticism and agnosticism made him a controversial figure, particularly in his native Scotland. His writings include *A Treatise of Human*

Nature (1738–40), *An Enquiry Concerning Human Understanding* (1748), *Dialogues Concerning Natural Religion* (published post-humously in 1779) and books about the history of Britain.

Hyphenated principles. Fletcher emphasizes the point that the situationist's concern is with application of the principle of love to concrete situations. He must not think of 'love' in isolation, but of how it relates to specific questions, such as school integration (black and white children attending the same school: a controversial issue in the United States in the 1950s and 1960s), or abortion.

Hypothetical imperatives. Kant distinguishes (*Groundwork of the Metaphysics of Morals*) between the imperatives of morality, which are always categorical, and hypothetical imperatives, which do not command absolutely, but only as a means of achieving another purpose.

Hypothetical (moral decisions). As each situation is unique, a decision made in one situation may not be the most loving in another, however closely the two situations resemble each other.

Impossibility of love. Reinhold Niebuhr (see below) argues that Jesus' love ethic, as expressed in the Sermon on the Mount, cannot be carried out in the world as it is, by sinful human beings. In his view it is an impossible ideal, whose role is to highlight the shortcomings of generally accepted ethical standards, which will encourage human beings to repent, and become recipients of God's grace.

Incarnation. The Christian teaching that in Jesus Christ God became incarnate (took on human form), in order to redeem human beings.

Intergroup relations. Relations between groups of people in society, as distinct from those between individuals.

Interim Committee. The committee appointed by President Truman to consider the question of whether or not to use atomic weapons against Japan. See also A-bombs on Hiroshima and Nagasaki above.

Internal spiritual or mystical affair. See Pietism below.

Interpersonal relationships. Relations between individuals.

Intrinsicalism. The view that some things are always good or bad, or right or wrong, irrespective of circumstances.

Intrinsicalist ethics. See intrinsicalism above.

Intuition theory or faculty theory of conscience. See Conscience above. Ethical intuitionism holds that goodness is a non-natural property of things, which people can only know through intuition. This was the view of the philosopher G. E. Moore (see below).

Glossary

James, William (1842–1910). American philosopher and psychologist, one of the founders of philosophical pragmatism, and brother of the novelist Henry James. After obtaining a medical degree from Harvard, James taught medicine there, while pursuing his interests in psychology, philosophy and the nature of religious belief, and became consecutively professor of philosophy and psychology. His books include *The Principles of Psychology* (1890), *The Varieties of Religious Experience* (1902) and *The Will to Believe* (1907). See also American pragmatism above.

Jesus' Summary. The Great Commandment, found in Mark 12.28–31, which is the fundamental principle of situation ethics. A scribe asks Jesus which is the most important commandment, and Jesus replies: "'The first is, 'Hear, O Israel: The Lord our God . . . is one; and you shall love . . . God with all your heart, and with all your soul, and with all your mind, and with all your strength.' The second is this, 'You shall love your neighbour as yourself.' There is no other commandment greater than these.'"

Kant, Immanuel (1724–1804). German philosopher, whose ideas on metaphysics, moral philosophy and the philosophy of religion have had a profound and lasting influence on thinking in all these areas. Kant devoted his life to philosophical reflection and writing, and was professor of logic and metaphysics at the University of Königsberg in East Prussia. His books include *Critique of Pure Reason* (1781 and 1787), *Groundwork of the Metaphysics of Morals* (1785) and *Critique of Practical Reason* (1788). Kant's approach to ethics differs sharply from that of situationism: see Kant's legalism below.

Kant's legalism. Kant's view that there are moral laws (see below), such as that lying is wrong, which must always be obeyed, irrespective of circumstances.

Kierkegaard, Søren (1813–55). Danish philosopher and theologian whose focus on the implications of religious belief and the individual's relationship with God for the individual led him to reject the prevailing Hegelian philosophy of the period, which made little of the individual. His preoccupation with the individual, individual choice and despair mean that he is regarded as the first existentialist (see Existentialism above) philosopher and writer. His books include *Fear and Trembling* (1843), *Philosophical Fragments* (1844) and *Practice in Christianity* (1850).

King, Martin Luther (1929–68). Baptist minister and civil rights campaigner. Born in Atlanta, Georgia, the son and grandson of Baptist ministers, he led the bus boycott in Montgomery, Alabama

(1955–56) which brought about desegregation of buses in the state. He co-ordinated the great civil rights march of a quarter of a million people on Washington in 1963, and his peaceful campaigning for civil rights across the United States contributed to the passing of civil rights legislation. He was awarded the Nobel Peace Prize in 1964, and was assassinated at Memphis, Tennessee, in April 1968.

Leahy, Admiral William Daniel (1875–1959). Chief of Naval Operations in the United States Navy and subsequently Governor of Puerto Rico and Ambassador to Vichy France. President Roosevelt appointed him his chief of staff during World War Two, to co-ordinate his relations with the heads of the three services. Leahy believed that Japan was ready to surrender, and opposed the use of atomic bombs in 1945. He thought that the United States was adopting 'an ethical standard common to the barbarians of the Dark Ages'.

Legalism/legalistic (approach to morals). The view that there are absolute ethical principles or rules which must always be followed, irrespective of circumstances.

Legalistic puritanism. The combination of moral legalism (see above) and a puritanical attitude, which in this case opposes abortion under any circumstances.

Legalistic reason. Reason working within the confines of absolute ethical principles or rules. See also Natural law below.

Lewis, Captain Robert A. (1918–83). Co-pilot of the *Enola Gay* (see above).

Lewis, Clive Staples (1898–1963). Specialist in medieval and renaissance literature who spent most of his academic career at Oxford, where he was fellow of Magdalen College, before becoming Professor of Medieval and Renaissance English at Cambridge. An active Christian, Lewis was a popular writer and broadcaster about Christianity and the author of children's books. His books include *Allegory of Love* (1936), *The Screwtape Letters* (1942), *Mere Christianity* (1952) and the *Chronicles of Narnia* (1950–56). The quotation is from *The Four Loves* (1960).

Libertinism. A practitioner of antinomian ethics (see above) and/or one who is sexually promiscuous.

Life, death and resurrection of Jesus Christ. See Grace, the new life in Christ and salvation by faith above.

Love canon alone. Ethics based on love. See Jesus' Summary above.

Love ethic. Ethics based on love. See Jesus' Summary above.

Love God in the neighbour. See Jesus' Summary above.

Glossary

Love has more control of law. In Sweden, there were more liberal abortion laws than in the United States, which took full account of the interests and wishes of the pregnant woman.

Man-to-God and man-to-man dimensions. In relation to carrying out the Great Commandment (see Jesus' Summary above) and loving God and our neighbours.

Maquis. The name given to the French resistance groups during World War Two. The term originates from the small scrub bushes in the forests where they took refuge.

Matthew 5.43–48. In this passage of the Sermon on the Mount, Jesus contrasts his teaching about love with that of the Old Testament Law. The latter had limited it to love for the neighbour, whereas Jesus instructs his followers to: 'Love your enemies and pray for those who persecute you, so that you may be sons of your Father who is in heaven.'

Maximal sense. In the sense of the greatest quantity.

Maxims, never rules. A principle which guides conduct, but which may be deemed inappropriate in a particular situation, as opposed to an inflexible rule.

McCarthy, Joseph (1908–57). American lawyer and politician. After serving as a circuit judge in Wisconsin, and in the Marines during World War Two, McCarthy was elected to the US Senate (1946), where he became chairman of the Committee on Government Operations (1953). During the 1950s he made frequent, but unsubstantiated, allegations of communist infiltration of the US government and army.

Medical social security legislation. The United States does not provide its citizens with universal healthcare, free at the point of use.

Metaphysics. Study of what is after (beyond) physics, and which cannot be investigated by ordinary empirical methods; the investigation of what really exists, of ultimate reality. It can also refer (sometimes pejoratively) to philosophical systems which attempt to explain the nature of ultimate reality, and for which, although they may be coherent, there is little or no empirical evidence. Thus, at the end of his *An Enquiry Concerning Human Understanding*, the empirical philosopher David Hume (see above) humorously suggests that books about theology and metaphysics should be consigned to the flames.

Mill, John Stuart (1806–73). British utilitarian and empiricist philosopher, social reformer, East India Company administrator and Liberal MP, whose writings, which include *On Liberty* (1859),

Utilitarianism (1861) and *The Subjection of Women* (1869), have had a major and continuing influence on moral and political philosophy, as well as on thinking about the rights of individuals and minorities, and the relationship between the individual and the state.

Monolithic and jealous standard, a univalent norm. See *Agape* and Jesus' Summary above.

Moore, George Edward (1873–1958). British analytical and moral philosopher, who was professor of philosophy at Cambridge and whose books include *Principia Ethica* (1903), in which he puts forward an intuitionist theory of ethics (see above), *Ethics* (1912) and *Some Main Problems of Philosophy* (1953).

Moral law. A strict/inflexible moral principle or rule and also Kant's term for the *a priori* (not learned from experience) moral principles, discovered by the reason, which should always govern the actions of all rational beings.

Moral norm. Moral standard or rule.

Moral theology. See Catholic moral theology/theologian above.

Moralism. Fletcher's term for an approach to morality which focuses on breaches of petty rules, for example those about Sunday observance, but ignores major violations of the ethic of love, such as inequality and injustice.

National Association for the Advancement of Colored People (NAACP). Organization formed in 1910 to campaign non-violently for civil rights for non-white Americans. One of its initial aims was to reduce the number of lynchings of black people in the United States.

Natural law. The ethical theory which holds that certain ethical principles and courses of action are good or right because they are consistent with the nature of human beings and the natural order, but that others are not. For many Christians, particularly Roman Catholics, natural law is the way that human beings, as rational beings, participate in the eternal law, by which God governs the universe, and they must base their ethical principles and decisions on it, in order to achieve their proper end as human beings, made in God's image.

Natural means or artificial insemination. Fletcher is challenging the orthodox Christian view that children should only be born within marriage and that non-natural methods of conception are unacceptable.

Neighbour-regarding. Focused on the welfare of the neighbour.

Neocasuistry. Situationism involves applying the love ethic to specific, concrete situations, so casuistry seems relevant. However, according to Fletcher, every situation is unique, so it is hard to see what use any form of casuistry would be to the situationist, as it involves working out detailed rules, in advance of a situation arising. The situationist can only decide how to act when he is confronted by the actual situation. See also Casuistry above.

Neuhaus, Dr Richard John (1936–2009). Canadian-born former Lutheran minister who converted to Roman Catholicism, and whose books include *The Catholic Moment* (1987) and *America Against Itself* (1992).

New morality. This is the term Fletcher and others, such as John Robinson (see below), use to refer to situation ethics.

Newman, Cardinal John Henry (1801–90). Fellow of Oriel College, Oxford, Anglican clergyman, and a leading member of the Oxford Movement, which held that the Church of England should be free of the state. Newman converted to Roman Catholicism, because he believed it was the only true Church. One of the leaders of the revival of Roman Catholicism in nineteenth-century Britain, Newman's writings covered a wide range of subjects, including education (*The Idea of a University*, 1852), his own religious life (*Apologia pro Vita Sua*, 1864) and philosophy of religion (*A Grammar of Assent*, 1870).

Niebuhr, Helmut Richard (1894–1962). Evangelical and Reformed Church pastor, Professor of Theology and Christian Ethics at Yale Divinity School and brother of Reinhold (see below). His books include *The Kingdom of God in America* (1937), which explores the role of the idea of the kingdom of God in the history of Protestantism in the United States, *The Meaning of Revelation* (1941) and *Christ and Culture* (1951).

Niebuhr, Reinhold (1892–1971). Evangelical and Reformed Church pastor, campaigner for social justice, Professor of Christian Ethics at Union Theological Seminary, New York and brother of Helmut (see above). Niebuhr believed that there are limits to what human beings and human society can achieve: a position known as Christian Realism. His books include *An Interpretation of Christian Ethics* (1934), in which he argues that sinfulness prevents human beings fulfilling the Sermon on the Mount's love ethic, *The Nature and Destiny of Man* (1941–43) and *Faith and History* (1949).

No logical bridge from facts to values, from isness to oughtness. In *A Treatise of Human Nature*, David Hume raises the question of the relationship between statements of fact ('is' statements) and statements of value ('ought' statements). He appears to suggest that

Glossary

a move from, for example, '*x* is suffering', to 'we ought to help *x*', is logically flawed, as no evaluation (what we ought to do) follows from any factual statement. According to some philosophers, we cannot move from a minor premise ('*x* is suffering') to a conclusion ('we ought to help *x*'), except by way of a major premise, such as 'we ought always to help those who are suffering'. However, the interpretation of the passage is still disputed.

No person or human life in an embryo at an early stage of pregnancy. This is the essence of the issue between supporters and opponents of abortion: what is the moral status of the embryo/foetus? Supporters of abortion take the view that Fletcher expresses here: that particularly just after conception an embryo is not even a sentient, much less a rational, being, and so has no, or very limited, moral status. Opponents maintain that as all the elements of the future human person are present, the embryo is entitled to the protection given to a human person.

Nominalistic. Here, that situation ethics recognizes no absolute ethical values, apart from love.

Non-maleficence. Non-hurtfulness, not harming others.

Nonmedically indicated abortions. Abortions in situations where there is no (serious) threat to the pregnant woman's health or life.

Non-reciprocal. The nature of *agape* (see above) love is that it is given without expectation of being returned.

Normative ethics. This concerns the objects or ends which we regard, or should regard, as good, and the rules or principles that we adopt, or ought to adopt, to govern and/or assess our conduct.

Normative relativism. See Ethical relativism above.

Omnified. Extended to all.

One and only universal law. See *Agape* and Jesus' Summary above.

Optimific. Intent on maximizing love.

Over-simplifying Tolstoyan idea. The view that Christians should not assess a situation carefully, in order to calculate how to produce most love, which may involve choosing who should receive it, but give it blindly to the nearest person.

Patriotic prostitution. Use sex, and so effectively turn herself into a prostitute, in order to serve her country.

Paul, Saint (believed to have died AD 64–68). Christian missionary and theologian, who, after his conversion to Christianity, dedicated his life to preaching Christianity to the Gentiles (non-Jews). Paul's letters or epistles to the Christian churches form part of the New Testament.

Glossary

Peirce, Charles Sanders (1839–1914) **(pp. oo–o)**. American philosopher, scientist/philosopher of science, logician, mathematician and founder of philosophical pragmatism. Peirce worked mainly for the United States Coast and Geodetic (mathematical study of the earth's area and distances) Survey and also taught mathematics at Johns Hopkins University, Baltimore. Peirce's papers were published in eight volumes, 1931–58.

Personalistic/personalism/personalist view. The view that nothing is valuable in itself, but derives its value (or lack of it) from whether or not it helps or harms persons.

Pharisees' principle of statutory morality. The Pharisees, or 'separated ones', were strict followers of the Jewish written and oral law. Jesus denounced them for being more interested in petty religious rules about such matters as food, ritual cleansing and Sabbath observance than important spiritual and ethical matters: 'Now you Pharisees cleanse the outside of the cup and of the dish, but inside you are full of extortion and wickedness' (Luke 11.39).

Philosophical systems. See Metaphysics above.

Pietism. When religion becomes purely a matter of the relationship between the believer and God, and loses its ethical dimension of how we should behave towards others and discharge our responsibilities to society.

Pleasure principle. The principle of utility: that actions are right to the extent that they promote pleasure and (the greatest) happiness, and wrong to the extent that they promote pain.

Positivism. See Theological positivism below.

Pragmatic-empirical temper (of situation ethics). See American pragmatism and British empiricism above.

Precepts of Torah. The rules of the Jewish Law, believed to have been given to Moses and found in the Pentateuch, the first five books of the Old Testament.

Principled relativism. Fletcher's term for his view that general ethical principles offer insights into, and guidance about, ethical decisions, but are not to be treated as definite ethical rules.

Re-creation as well as for procreation. Sex is for enjoyment, as well as procreation, and contraception makes it possible to enjoy sex without the risk of pregnancy.

Regulative principle of Christian ethics. Love: the fundamental principle, which governs the whole of Christian ethics.

Reifies good and evil. Objectifies good and evil, turning them into things-in-themselves, whereas 'good' and 'evil' are just ways of referring to actions or entities which help or harm human beings.

Relativistic (of ethics). See Ethical relativism above.

Religiosity. See Pietism above.

Robinson, Dr John Arthur Thomas (1919–83). New Testament scholar and Anglican clergyman, J. A. T. Robinson studied theology at Cambridge, where he became a lecturer and Dean of Chapel of Trinity College. As Bishop of Woolwich (1959–69), he aroused controversy with his book *Honest to God* (1963), in which he explored the nature of Christian theology and belief in the context of the work of Paul Tillich and Dietrich Bonhoeffer, and also wrote positively about Fletcher's approach to Christian ethics. His other books include *But That I Can't Believe* (1967) and *Redating the New Testament* (1976).

Romantic love (*eros*). The love felt for a husband/wife or sexual partner. See also *Agape* and Friendship love (*philia*) above.

Roosevelt, Franklin Delano (1882–1945). The thirty-second president (Democrat) of the United States (1933–45) and previously a senator, assistant secretary of the United States Navy in Woodrow Wilson's administration, and governor of New York. Through his New Deal programme, Roosevelt helped to revive the American economy following the Wall Street Crash and the Great Depression, and then led the United States successfully through World War Two.

Roosevelt, Theodore (1858–1919). The twenty-sixth president (Republican) of the United States (1901-09) and previously assistant secretary of the United States Navy in President McKinley's administration, governor of New York, and McKinley's vice president.

Rules of Sabbath observance. Jesus defied the numerous rules governing behaviour on the Sabbath, the day set aside in Jewish law for worship of God. On one occasion his disciples were plucking heads of grain to eat as they walked through a grainfield, and were criticized by the Pharisees for doing forbidden work on the sabbath. Jesus' response was: 'The sabbath was made for man, not man for the sabbath' (Mark 2.27).

Russell, Bertrand Arthur William, 3rd Earl Russell (1872–1970). British philosopher, mathematician, writer and peace campaigner, and grandson of Whig prime minister, Lord John Russell (1st Earl Russell). Fellow of Trinity College, Cambridge and author of *Principia Mathematica* (1910–13), *The Problems of Philosophy* (1912), *Why I Am Not a Christian* (1927) and *History of Western Philosophy* (1945).

Sanger, Margaret Higgins (1879–1966). American nurse and lifetime campaigner for contraception and birth control, who opened the first birth control clinic in the United States (1916) and founded the American Birth Control League (1921), which became the Planned Parenthood Federation (1942). Her books include *Family Limitation* (1914), *What Every Girl Should Know* (1920) and *The Pivot of Civilization* (1922).

Sartre, Jean-Paul (1905–80). French existentialist (see Existentialism above) philosopher, writer and playwright, whose works include *Nausea, Being and Nothingness* and the influential lecture *Existentialism and Humanism*. Fletcher draws attention to Sartre's view that there can be no general moral rules or principles.

Schizophrenic psychosis. A severe mental disorder which involves loss of contact with reality and withdrawal from contact with others.

Schweitzer, Albert (1875–1965). Theologian, philosopher, musicologist, organist, missionary and medical practitioner, who devoted his life, from 1913 until his death, to running a hospital in Africa. His books include *The Quest for the Historical Jesus* (1910), *On the Edge of the Primeval Forest* (1922) and *Out of My Life and Thought* (1931).

Second maxim (second formulation of the categorical imperative). This is: 'So act that you use humanity, whether in your own person or in the person of any other, always at the same time as an end, never merely as a means' (Kant, *Groundwork of the Metaphysics of Morals*).

Self-realization. Morality involves duties to the self, as well as to others. In his *The Nicomachean Ethics*, Aristotle argues that human beings, who are rational beings, achieve *eudaimonia* (happiness/well-being) by practising the intellectual (developing their minds) and moral (fulfilling their duties to others) virtues.

Sermon on the Mount. The great collection of Jesus' ethical teachings in Matthew 5—7. See also collection of scattered sayings and editor-compiler of Matthew's Sermon on the Mount above.

Situation ethicist. Ethicist who teaches and/or practises situationism.

Situational variables. All the morally relevant factors in a particular situation.

Situationism, contextualism and circumstantialism. Different terms for the situationist approach to ethics, which involves assessing all the morally relevant factors of each individual situation.

Source principle. Fundamental principle.

Statutory system of rules. Absolute rules, which must always be observed: a view wholly opposed to situationism.

Glossary

Sterilization. Surgical procedure to prevent male or female reproducing.

Stranger-neighbour. Strangers are neighbours, because they are fellow human beings.

Strategic principle of the greatest good of the greatest number. See pleasure principle and consequentialist ethic above.

Summum bonum. The highest good, which, for Christian situationists, is (the maximization of) love.

Supernaturalistic legalism. The view that there are God-given rules, such as the Ten Commandments, which must not be broken in any situation.

Tawney, Richard Henry (1880–1962). Economic historian, Christian socialist and pioneer of adult education, who was Professor of Economic History at the London School of Economics (1931–49) and President of the Workers' Education Association (1928–44). His books include *Secondary Education for All* (1922), *Religion and the Rise of Capitalism* (1926) and *Equality* (1931).

Teleological ethic. *Telos* is the Greek for 'end' or 'purpose', so an ethic which aims at achieving a particular end or good. See also Consequentialist ethic.

Temple, William (1881–1944). Anglican clergyman, theologian, educationist and social reformer, who was bishop of Manchester (1921–29) and Archbishop of York (1929–42) and Canterbury (1942–44). His books include *Christianity and the State* (1928) and *Readings in St John's Gospel* (1939).

Ten Commandments. The moral rules that God gave to Moses on Mount Sinai. See Exodus 20.1–17.

Thalidomide. A drug developed during the 1950s which was prescribed to pregnant women to combat morning sickness and as a sedative, but which caused severe birth defects in children.

Theological positivism. Faith is a matter of will and choice. People do not, in Fletcher's opinion, arrive at belief in God's existence as the result of a process of rational argument. They start with the conviction that God exists, or choose to believe that he does, and then use reason to work out what faith in God means, and how it should affect the way they behave towards others.

Theology of situation ethics. That God is love, and reason is merely love's instrument. See also *Agape* above.

Therapeutic abortions. See Abortion above.

Tillich, Paul Johannes (1886–1965). German theologian and Lutheran minister, who was professor at Marburg, Dresden and Leipzig,

Glossary

before being banned from teaching by the Nazis, and moving to the United States, where he was professor at Union Theological Seminary, New York and Harvard and Chicago Divinity Schools. His work is controversial, as he treats religious belief as ultimate concern with the ground of our being. His books include *Systematic Theology* (1951–63) and *The Courage to Be* (1952).

Tolstoy, Count Leo Lev Nikolayevich (1828–1910). Writer, social reformer, landowner and author of the novels *War and Peace* (1869) and *Anna Karenina* (1877). Tolstoy's views on Jesus' teaching on the Sermon on the Mount are set out in *What I Believe* (1883).

Treat persons always as ends, never merely as means. See Second maxim (second formulation of the categorical imperative) above.

Truman, Harry S. (1884–1972). The thirty-third president (Democrat) of the United States (1945–53), who was previously a senator for Missouri and Franklin D. Roosevelt's vice president. Truman knew nothing about Project Manhattan (the development of atomic weapons) before becoming president. His presidency saw the creation of the United Nations and NATO, and the Marshall Plan: US aid which helped with European economic reconstruction after World War Two.

United Mine Workers of America (UMWA). Founded in 1890, the union represents miners and other industrial workers in the United States.

Universals and the categorical imperative. Moral rules or laws which apply universally, irrespective of the situation. See Categorical imperative and Moral law above.

Unlovingness of law-bound conscience. Those who believe that there are absolute ethical rules will be unable to apply the love ethic (see above) fully.

Unwanted and unintended baby. Fletcher argues for non-therapeutic abortions (see Abortion above), on the grounds of the undesirable consequences for the child itself, the family and society, when unintended and unwanted children are born.

Utilitarian(ism). See Consequentialist ethic, Bentham and Mill above.

Valid natural moral laws. See Natural law above.

Virtue. Moral excellence, a positive character trait which makes someone morally good and admirable. See also Aristotle above.

Wedge principle. Here, that allowing a moral rule to be broken will lead to further breaches and ultimately general disobedience of it.

While we were yet sinners Christ died for us. In Romans 5.8, Paul explains that God showed his love for human beings by sending Jesus to die on their behalf, while they were still sinners. See also Incarnation above.

Index

A-bombs on Hiroshima and
    Nagasaki 14, 21–2, 53, 68,
    79, 89, 91, 99, 103
abortion 2, 6–7, 38, 60–1, 66,
    71, 84–5, 88, 91, 102, 104–5,
    108–9, 113, 114
active determination of the will
    53, 80, 91
acquaintance-neighbour 29,
    54, 91
advisers without veto power
    (ethical principles as) 42, 91
agape 5, 8, 11–4, 20, 22, 25–6,
    28–9, 33, 36–7, 40–1, 45–6,
    48, 50, 52–6, 70, 72, 76, 78,
    80, 91–5, 100, 106, 109–10, 113
agapeic calculus 22, 29, 52–3,
    79, 92
agapeic love 8, 11, 14, 20, 26,
    50, 56, 72, 91–3
aggressive, questing prudence of
    agape 48, 92–3
altruistic 55, 81, 92
American pragmatism 39, 92,
    103, 110
Anglo-American principle of
    minding your own business
    48, 92–3
antecedent rather than
    consequent conscience 42, 93

antinomian (approach to morals)
    3–5, 34–6, 69–70, 93, 97, 105
arbitrary and absurd as the leap
    of faith 40–1, 93
Aristotle 37, 93, 101, 112, 114
artificial insemination 58, 61,
    82, 85, 93, 107
Augustine, Saint 47, 93
axiomatic value 41, 93

backbone of all legalism 45,
    93–4
Barth, Karl 63, 94
Be all-inclusive in your *agape* as
    God is in his 54, 81, 94
Be perfect as your heavenly
    Father is (Matthew 5.48) 14,
    54, 94
benevolence 14, 45, 54, 80, 94,
    100
Bentham, Jeremy 8, 13, 52, 92,
    94, 101, 114
biblical revelation 35, 70, 94
bioethics 2, 94
Bonhoeffer, Dietrich 8, 21, 39,
    63, 94, 101, 110–1
British empiricism 39, 95, 110
Brunner, Emil 36, 51, 63, 95

casuistry 19, 34, 63, 65, 86, 95,
    107

categorical (moral decisions) 36, 95

categorical imperative 9, 41, 58, 95, 102, 112, 114

Catholic moral theology/ theologian 35, 38, 51, 69, 91, 95, 106

chastity 45, 95

c-love 33, 95

Christian sex relations (marital monopoly) 48, 96

Churchill, Winston 68, 96

classical moralists 45, 96

classical pacifism 12, 48, 96

coexistence of its means and ends puts it in the realm of ethics 56, 96

collection of scattered sayings 28, 47, 96, 98

conscience (moral consciousness) as a function not a faculty 9, 27–8, 36, 42, 45, 48–9, 51, 60, 73, 93, 96, 103, 114

consequentialist ethic 13, 52, 79, 94, 97, 112–4

context/contextual particularity 19, 28, 33, 37, 42, 49, 59–63, 73, 83, 85, 97, 100, 112

contributory hierarchy 58, 97

I Corinthians 6: 12–20 35, 97, 101

Cox, Harvey 30, 97

created men in his own image 41, 97, 99

Cummings, e.e. 33, 97

deontological ethics 13, 52, 79, 97–8

dispositions of the will 54, 98

divine command 54, 98

Dodd, C.H. 53, 98

dogmatism 45, 98

editor-compiler of Matthew's Sermon on the Mount 54, 98, 112

enemy-neighbour 14, 29, 54, 81, 99

Enola Gay 68, 99

Episcopal Church 1–2, 99

ethical relativism 40, 61, 72, 99, 109–10

eugenics 2, 99

euthanasia 2, 58, 63, 99

existentialism 36, 99, 104, 111–2

extrinsicalism of situation ethics 45, 74, 100

faith propositions are affirmed voluntaristically 40, 100

faith working through love 41, 100

free contextual choices 28, 49, 100

friend-neighbour 54, 81, 100

friendship love (*philia*) 48, 100, 110

fruits of the Spirit 54, 100

Gnostics 4, 35, 100

God is love 8, 25–6, 41, 44, 72, 74, 100, 113

grace and freedom 4, 20, 25, 35, 40, 59, 63, 86, 94, 100–2, 105

grace, the new life in Christ and salvation by faith 35, 101, 105

Hare, R. M. 6, 30, 101

Index

Hatfield, Forrest 2, 101

hedonistic/hedonic calculus (or felicific calculus) 13, 29, 52, 79, 92, 101

history of western morals 34, 101

Hitler, Adolf (plot to kill) 6, 37, 94, 101

homosexuality 18, 34, 61, 85, 101–2

Hume, David 8, 31, 41, 95, 102, 106, 108

hyphenated principles 66, 88, 102

hypothetical imperatives 58, 102

hypothetical (moral decisions) 19, 36, 85, 102

impossibility of love 44, 102

incarnation 64–5, 87, 102, 114

intergroup relations 51, 102

Interim Committee 68, 102–3

internal spiritual or mystical affair 65, 103

interpersonal relationships 51, 103

intrinsicalism 16–7, 23, 45, 57–8, 75, 82–3, 93–4, 96, 100, 103

intrinsicalist ethics 45, 103

intuition or faculty theory of conscience 36, 103

James, William 39, 92, 103

Jesus' Summary 2–3, 52, 61, 103

Kant, Immanuel 9, 41, 44–5, 73, 95, 98, 1024, 106, 112

Kant's legalism 45, 103–4

Kierkegaard, Sören 39, 104

King, Martin Luther 61, 104

Leahy, Admiral William 68, 104

legalism/legalistic (approach to morals) 3–5, 10, 12, 18, 34–5, 37–8, 45, 47–9, 57, 64–6, 69–71, 75–7, 87–8, 93–4, 99, 103–4, 112

legalistic puritanism 35, 104

legalistic reason 35, 104

Lewis, Captain Robert A. 68, 104

Lewis, C. S. 64, 104–5

libertinism 35, 105

life, death and resurrection of Jesus Christ 64, 87, 105

love canon alone 27–8, 105

love ethic 3,5, 22, 37–8, 52–3, 55, 60, 79, 81, 84, 92, 96, 102, 105, 107–8, 114

love God in the neighbour 36, 105

love has more control of law 60, 105

man-to-God and man-to-man dimensions 54, 105

Maquis 57, 105

Matthew 5: 43–48 54, 99, 105

maximal sense 54, 105

maxims, never rules 42, 105

McCarthy, Joseph 1, 105–6

medical social security legislation 66, 88, 106

metaphysics 39, 103, 106, 110

Mill, John Stuart 8, 13, 22, 31, 40, 52, 114

monolithic and jealous standard, a univalent norm 46, 106

Index

Moore, G. E. 16–7, 22, 31, 63,
  103
moral law   4, 35, 40, 46, 49,
  59–60, 62, 69–70, 84, 103,
  106, 114
moral norm 36, 65, 95, 106
moral theology 34, 65, 95, 106
moralism 65–7, 87–8, 106

National Association for the
  Advancement of Colored
  People 66, 107
natural law 4, 35–6, 47, 69, 76,
  94, 104, 107, 114
natural means or artificial
  insemination 58, 82, 107
neighbour-regarding 28, 76,
  107
neocasuistry 63, 86, 107
Neuhaus, Richard 24, 31, 107
new morality 23, 28, 33, 47, 57,
  64, 76, 82, 86, 107
Newman, J. H. 35, 96, 107–8
Niebuhr, H.R. 44, 57, 108
Niebuhr, Reinhold 12, 44, 51,
  102, 107
no logical bridge from facts to
  values, from isness to
  oughtness 41, 108
no person or human life in an
  embryo at an early stage of
  pregnancy 7, 38, 71, 108
nominalistic 43, 108
non-maleficence 22, 92, 108
non-medically indicated
  abortions 60, 109
nonreciprocal 11, 28, 48, 76,
  109
normative (ethics) 3, 33, 40, 63,
  69, 109
normative relativism 26, 45, 109

omnified 50, 109
one and only universal law 36,
  109
optimific 27, 44, 50, 109
over-simplifying Tolstoyan idea
  50, 109

patriotic prostitution 67, 109
Paul, Saint 35, 40–2, 46, 54–5,
  63, 97, 100, 109
Peirce, Charles 92, 109
personalistic/personalism/
  personalist view 9, 33, 41–3,
  72, 109
Pharisees' principle of statutory
  morality 40, 66, 109, 111
philosophical systems 39, 106,
  110
pietism 65–6, 87–8, 103,
  109–10
pleasure principle 13, 52, 110,
  112
positivism 8, 40, 72, 100, 110
pragmatic-empirical temper (of
  situation ethics) 42, 110
precepts of Torah 46, 110
principled relativism 5, 37, 110

re-creation as well as for
  procreation 61, 110
regulative principle of Christian
  ethics 44, 74, 110
reifies good and evil 45, 110
relativistic (of ethics) 39, 110
religiosity 65, 110
Robinson, J.A.T. 23, 31, 33, 64,
  107, 110
romantic love (eros) 48, 110
Roosevelt, Franklin 68, 104,
  110–1, 114
Roosevelt, Theodore 57, 111

rules of Sabbath observance 11,
    46, 111
Russell, Bertrand 4, 35, 64, 111

Sanger, Margaret 2, 111
Sartre, Jean-Paul 36, 70, 111
schizophrenic psychosis 6, 38,
    111
Schweitzer, Albert 48, 112
second maxim (second
    formulation of the categorical
    imperative) 44, 112, 114
self-realization 37, 112
Sermon on the Mount 11, 14,
    28, 47, 54, 96, 98, 102, 105,
    108, 112–3
situation ethicist 13, 16, 18, 20,
    35, 42. 48, 76, 92, 95–7, 112
situational variables 37, 70,
    112
situationism, contextualism and
    circumstantialism 27, 46, 75,
    112
source principle 47, 76, 112
statutory system of rules 27,
    46, 75, 112
sterilization 2, 61, 85, 112
stranger-neighbour 14, 29, 54,
    112
strategic principle of the greatest
    good of the greatest number
    52, 112
summum bonum 39, 58, 112
supernaturalistic legalism 64,
    112

Tawney, R.H. 1, 113

teleological ethic 13, 52, 113
Temple, William 2, 37, 51, 113
Ten Commandments 11, 21,
    46–7, 75, 112–3
thalidomide 60, 84, 113
theological positivism 40, 100,
    110, 113
theology of situation ethics 44,
    113
therapeutic abortions 38, 113–4
Tillich, Paul 40, 110, 113
Tolstoy, Leo 50, 56, 109, 113
treat persons always as ends,
    never merely as means 41,
    73, 113–4
Truman, Harry S. 14, 21, 53,
    68, 79, 89, 91, 96, 102, 114

United Mine Workers of
    America 1, 114
universals and the categorical
    imperative 58, 114
unlovingness of law-bound
    conscience 45, 114
unwanted and unintended baby
    24, 35, 38, 71, 114
utilitarian(ism) 8, 13–4, 16, 22,
    40, 52, 72, 79, 92, 94, 97,
    106, 114
valid natural moral laws 4, 35,
    114
virtue 4, 51, 54, 61, 85, 93, 100,
    112, 114

wedge principle 58, 114
while we were yet sinners Christ
    died for us 54–5, 114